PRAISE for *A Passion for the Past*

Jim Percoco is a highly talented teacher of long experience. He is spirited, full of ideas, often original in approach. But the real secret of the Percoco classroom magic is that unbeatable combination of a love of teaching and an all-out love of his subject. With so much of the teaching of history so sadly and so unnecessarily in the doldrums, his lively new book couldn't be more welcome.

—David McCullough

Jim Percoco's *A Passion for the Past* is an educational manifesto that should be read by all Americans. Teachers and parents alike should use it as a springboard to explore the joyous new ways to rediscover our national heritage.

—Douglas Brinkley, author of *The Majic Bus: An American Odyssey* and Director of the Eisenhower Center for American Studies at the University of New Orleans

Jim Percoco has a passion for American history and a gift for engaging his students in remarkably creative ways. His enthusiasm shines through every page. Everyone who teaches American history can benefit from his experiences, and perhaps I will not be alone in wishing to spend a year in his class watching history come alive.

—Edward T. Linenthal, author of *Preserving Memory: The Struggle to Create America's Holocaust Museum*, and coeditor of *History Wars: The* Enola Gay *and Other Battles for the American Past*

In *A Passion for the Past*, both new and experienced history teachers will find many models to draw upon for renewable inspiration for their profession as well as a wealth of compelling, often moving, activities that are practical for both teacher and student.

—Paul Gagnon, School of Education, Boston University

A Passion for the Past

A Passion for the Past

Creative Teaching of U.S. History

James A. Percoco

HEINEMANN
PORTSMOUTH, NH

Heinemann
A division of Reed Elsevier Inc.
361 Hanover Street
Portsmouth, NH 03801–3912
http://www.heinemann.com

Offices and agents throughout the world

The author and publisher wish to thank those who have generously given permission to reprint borrowed material:

Excerpt from *The Killer Angels* by Michael Shaara. Copyright © 1974 by Michael Shaara. Reprinted by permission of Random House, Inc.

Excerpt from *Marching Through Georgia: My Walk with Sherman* by Jerry Ellis. Copyright © 1995 by Jerry Ellis. Used by permission of Delacorte Press, a division of Bantam Doubleday Dell Publishing.

Excerpts from *The Last Full Measure: The Life and Death of the First Minnesota Volunteers* by Richard Moe, © 1993 by Richard Moe. Reprinted by permission of Henry Holt and Company, Inc.

Figure 7-1 Antietam Memorial Illumination, photo courtesy of Judi Quelland, Valley Studio, Williamsport, MD.

Library of Congress Cataloging-in-Publication Data
Percoco, James A.
  A passion for the past : creative teaching of U.S. history / James A. Percoco.
    p.   cm.
  Includes bibliographical references (p. 143).
  ISBN 0-325-00061-1 (alk. paper)
  1. United States—History—Study and teaching (Middle school) 2. United States—History—Study and teaching (Secondary) I. Title.
E175.8.P47   1998
973'.071'273—dc21
                                                                98-21451
                                                                CIP

Editor: William Varner

Printed in the United States of America on acid-free paper
05 04 03 02   DA   7 8 9 10

This book is lovingly dedicated to the memory of my grandfather
Anthony DiLieto.
Though he only had an eighth-grade education, he was one of the finest teachers I ever
had.
Thanks Poppie!

Contents

Foreword

Fifty years ago, near the end of my high school studies, I sat in the class of a trim, organized teacher of U.S. history. He liked the subject, he cared for his students, and he assigned David Muzzey's *American History*—arguably the best available textbook at the time in terms of its lively presentation, wry humor, and up-to-date scholarship. My teacher didn't tell me any lies; he taught only what he knew, which was mostly in the textbook.

I appreciated the teacher's sure hand and knowing air, but the class left me cold. I ditched it regularly to sneak off to the high school newspaper office where I wrote stories for the sports page. Since I turned in my homework assignments and did reasonably well on tests, the history teacher let me alone. Perhaps the faculty advisor to the newspaper asked my history teacher to overlook my absences.

This was a few years after the end of World War II. None of us suspected that the chances of bringing history alive to teenagers depended heavily on going beyond a fat textbook. Teachers lived by textbooks; we were tested on textbooks. Living just outside Philadelphia, American history was all around us. My high school was about equidistant from Valley Forge and Independence Hall and surrounded by the land settled by William Penn's Quaker settlers. Yet we went to no historic sites to imagine how Washington's army nearly froze to death in the brutal winter of 1777–78 or how fifty-five delegates contrived the Constitution in Philadelphia in the sweltering summer of 1787. Nor did we visit historical societies or museums. We saw no history-based movies, we knew of no historical reenactments. We listened to no period music, gazed upon no historical monuments, had no classroom visitors who might relate their own experiences about history they had lived through. We did not read historical novels, and our teacher showed us no art, architecture, or photography to bring alive the past. History was cool—cool, that is, in the meaning of that word half a century ago. It was tepid, not passionate; it was detached, not engaged; it was cerebral, not emotional. I didn't like it. If asked why, I wouldn't have presented much of an answer.

Jim Percoco is a cool teacher (in today's student parlance) because he has adopted a "hands-on and student-centered" approach to the past that carries history education outside the classroom and beyond the textbook.

His mission also rests on the notion that history "is subject to interpretation and that we all perceive the same thing from different viewpoints." In this how-to-do-it book, he opens up his teaching kit for teachers everywhere to see why students at his high school jostle for a place in his classes. It is quite a kit.

This book on applied history is not based on a discovery that a radical new pedagogy can engage young students in history. Rather, Percoco has improved upon a venerable pedagogy. On the eve of World War I, John W. Wayland, a professor of history education at State Normal School in Harrisonburg, Virginia, counseled neophyte teachers that "we remember one tenth of what we hear, five tenths of what we see, and nine tenths of what we do." Upon his premise, Wayland stressed "the visual appeal in the teaching of history," the potential of historical reenactments, and the need for teachers to gather pictures, newspaper clippings, advertisements, picture postcards, postage stamps, and anything else that would show students how people lived and acted in past times.

In *How to Teach American History: A Handbook for Teachers and Students,* Wayland also provided a thirty-four-point list of "bad points that pupils have observed in history teachers." Among them were "not enough class discussion," "too much attention to small incidents," "not enough historical excursions," "not very enthusiastic over history," and "depending entirely on the textbook." As readers will see, Percoco agrees entirely with this nearly century-old antidote for the history blahs.

Why is it that American kids can't measure up to their peers in other countries, whether in science, math, or history? In fact, we drag the bottom in most global comparisons. No simple answer can be offered to this problem. One part of the difficulty seems certain. Teachers are inadequately trained. In history classrooms across the nation about half the teachers behind the big desks have only an undergraduate minor in history or not even that. Many are trained hardly at all in the subject they teach. Moving from U.S. to world history, the situation is even worse.

Another difficulty is that American teenagers work far more than their counterparts in other countries. But perhaps most disturbing is that students are too often served up a thin gruel in school classrooms. Recent annual surveys of 700,000 college-bound teenagers shows that nearly three-quarters of them believe that their classes were not academically rigorous. About the same percentage of teachers agree.

A good dose of Percoco's elixir cannot solve all of these problems, but most assuredly it can help. Ten years ago, in *And Sadly Teach: Teacher Education and Professionalism in American Culture* (1989), Jurgen Herbst lamented the lack of discipline-based teacher training and argued that "Teachers must take . . . responsibility for their own and their colleagues' professional development." Percoco has done just this. He understands that in many ways opportunities to teach history brilliantly have never been better. How so? First, textbooks have never been more balanced and inclusive, treating major parts of human populations, including women and racial minorities, that former textbooks ignored. Textbooks are also more interdisciplinary, visually stimulating, and challenging. Second, beyond the textbooks, the resources for engaging students are staggeringly rich. Never have so many historical societies and museums, forging new alliances between historian and curators, mounted so many fascinating hands-on exhibits. Walk through the Smithsonian's National Museum of American History or through your local historical society and see for yourself. Never before have teachers had available so many rich and historically sophisticated movies and television series. Before the 1900s, nobody had at their fingertips the millions of photographs, paintings, sculptures, buildings, primary documents, film clips, and secondary readings that spring onto one's computer screen through thousands of Internet websites. Third, we have witnessed in recent years the building of bridges between history educators in the schools, history educators in the universities, and history educators in historical societies, at historical sites, and in historical movie-making studios. Summer history workshops and colloquia have brought teacher-historians together where new historical knowledge and innovative teaching methods flow reciprocally across what has been a sharply drawn line. Academic historians have joyfully worked with museum curators and Hollywood scriptwriters to present history to the public outside the schoolhouse.

In short, history education is poised to be richer and more engaging as never before. The author of this book shows how to turn this potential into reality. He urges teaching colleagues "to nurture inside yourself the teacher that you want to be." Through down-to-earth descriptions of his own experiences and explorations with students, he demonstrates that the world beyond the schoolhouse door is an infinitely expandable textbook. He shows how to obliterate the line between academic historians in the universities and the history educators in the schools. A boundary crosser by nature, he arranges phone conversations so his students can talk with scholarly historians. He takes them where history was made and brings makers of history into the classroom. On the phone, on the road, online, and on fire, Percoco has caught himself up in transforming history education in his high school. Here, in 149 pages, he provided a crash course on what schools of education don't teach: how to become a professional history teacher.

Gary B. Nash

Acknowledgments

What a mystery is life! How could it be that I, now at the midpoint of my career as an educator, find myself writing a book? I know my old college roommates are about as surprised as I am because twenty years ago, as a senior graduating from college, I couldn't write very well. Ask my Dad! I can still picture him breathing down my back as I tried to put a paper together on Machiavelli's *The Prince* for my Political Philosophy course. What a difference twenty years makes! I've tried to sit back and figure out how so much in life has come together for me as a teacher. The only place I seem to be able to find an answer is when I lift my eyes in prayer, because what has happened to me since I first set foot in the classroom is nothing short of miraculous. And so my story as a teacher owes its first debt to God, who in only God's wisdom presented me with this precious gift. Rather than wait until the end of the acknowledgments I figure it would be best to start at the top. It seems that the Good Lord paved my way with the right people because there is no doubt in my mind just how blessed I have been to encounter all of the people I have met on my still unfolding pilgrimage—colleagues in and out of school as well as many of the students who I have enjoyed teaching. Some of these people you will meet in the following pages. Nevertheless, I need to thank everyone who has in some measure supported my work as a teacher as well as the writing of this book. For starters, let me begin with my father, Gerard Percoco, who often advised me as a youngster that he didn't care what I did with my life so long as it made me happy. Thanks Dad! I'm very happy! To my mother, Marilyn Percoco, for endless hours on her own hot line to the celestial realm! To my brothers Gregg, Stephen, and Anthony, as well as my sisters Gerilyn and Marilyn, though we're miles apart and all following different calls you've still made a difference. To my wonderful wife, Gina, who often has tried to figure out why her "crazy" husband has to traipse over every square inch of a historic site. Thanks for giving me the freedom to find my particular connection with the past. To my daughters Stephanie and Claire, who laugh with me when I play the soundtrack from *Gettysburg* and come down the steps dressed in a Civil War uniform. Just wait until you two are students at West Springfield High School.

Beyond my family there are those who in my college and early years helped to sustain my vision, particularly the gang at Yorktown Apartments 202 East and Bill Falone and Allison Rogers. My good friends of twenty plus years Tom DiNardo and Peter Bergh continue to be a source of support as are Kim and Reggie Harris and Fran Donnelly. Thanks for being there when the chips were down as well as when the sun's been bright.

In preparation for my journey as a teacher I offer thanks to my two mentors: Neal Adams, for his insiration as my high school history teacher, and Jerome Segal for a great five months as his student teacher. I'm glad that despite the years we're still in touch.

My wonderful colleagues of the West Springfield High School Social Studies department deserve a round of applause. They are in the best sense of the words professional and incredibly talented. On another level they have to deal with what some call my "never waning enthusiasm," as well as contending with my nefarious puns—all intended! But in particular to Jamie Morris, though now a fellow social studies teacher, was once a book publisher and who, without his ardent help and support, this project would never have been completed.

Former principal Glynn Bates deserves a word of thanks as she let me run with my dream of starting the Applied History class as does my current principal, Dr. David Smith, who continues to sustain the dream and vision. Dr. Smith also read portions of the manuscript and offered helpful suggestions. Other members of the West Springfield High School community who deserve thanks for having read portions of the book or providing solid input and support; they include Martha Chandler, Linda Vretos, Peggy Weidner, Carolyn Foronda, Susan Latour, and Judy Noun. Educators who work either in other schools or at the Fairfax County Department of Instructional Services that have also earned my thanks are Helena Bratten, Leslie Gray, Tim Hudenberg, Pat Donahue, Linda Miller, Bernie Glaze, and Mike Wildasin. Teachers from beyond the boundaries of Fairfax County, Virginia, who had some input include Grace Caporino, Paul Steuwe, and John Tyler. A majority of the photographs that illustrate this work were taken by my student Travis Washburn to whom I also owe my hearty thanks.

I will always be in debt to my good friends at the National Archives, Wynell Schammel and Rick Blondo. Thanks for making part of the journey with me and "primarily" keeping me focused. Also at the National Archives, my thanks to archivist Stuart Butler, who has filled my numerous requests regarding primary source material related to Andersonville Prison, and to Rita Sexton whose office has accommodated me and my students as they have prepared to conduct their primary search research. At the National Park Service I've met and worked with a great many soul mates, including the indefatigable former Chief Historian Ed Bearss, who has so generously given of his time and talent to me and my students, as has current Chief Historian, Dr. Dwight Pitcaithley. My good friend Beth

Boland, Head of the Teaching with Historic Places program, Susan Frisch-Lehrer at Chesterwood, John Dryfhout and Greg Schwarz of Saint-Gaudens National Historic Site, and Fred Boyles and Alan Marsh of Andersonville National Historic Site, and Marty Blatt of Boston National Historical Park have been a joy to work with and they understand the value of teachers and public historians working together. Alan, thanks for being a pun soul mate. At least somebody understands!

Thanks to author and historian David McCullough. First for your wonderful books that serve as an inspiration to my teaching. Most importantly, however, for your kindness to my students, me, and my mission. Also, thanks to Ed Linenthal and Brian Pohanka for their help and continuing support. At the National Council for History Education, Executive Director Elaine Reed has supported this project from its inception.

Thanks to Dr. Michael Richman for sharing his extensive knowledge on American public sculpture and for giving me the "eyes" one needs to evaluate such works of art. Also thanks to Susan Nichols, director of the Save Outdoor Sculpture project, who has worked with me for a number of years in the arena of outdoor sculpture. Also thanks to Amy Gross of the Pioneer Woman Museum in Ponca City, Oklahoma.

I also owe a big thanks to my neighbor, Jim Frost, who shepherded me through three down computer motherboards and answered my innumerable questions about computer applications. Having you a phone call away has made life in the Percoco household much easier. In addition, I'd like to also thank Dr. David Kobrin for his friendship and support as well as Marjorie Bingham for her constructive criticism of the manuscript. The book works quite nicely because of your contributions. Also, thanks to historian Dr. Pat Harahan, a member of the Springfield community who is an ardent supporter of my work.

A very special thanks goes to a number of World War II veterans who have shared their combat or prison experiences with me and my students. The men of Omaha Beach and Company A include Ray Nance, Bob Sales, Roy Stevens, Bob Slaughter, and Pride Wingfield. Those who spent time behind barbed wire in either Germany or Japan include Wayne Hitchcock, Bill Rolen, Doug Idlett, Carl Hedin, and the late Bill Troy. I hope that this book, in some small measure, can serve as a kind of payment from me, for what these men endured over fifty years ago on behalf of our nation. Ellen Wandrei, curator/manager of the Bedford City/County Museum, has been most helpful in assisting me with my research into Bedford and its role on D-Day.

No set of acknowledgments would be complete without a nod to my good friend at the Octagon Museum, Curator of Prints and Drawings, Sherry Birk. I can't imagine the '90s without you. Also a big thanks to my two George Washington University graduate interns, Angie Dodson and Rachel Teck. Sorry about the puns!

At Heinemann an important thank-you to my editor Bill Varner for sticking with me and for helping to make this book so much better than I ever could have imagined possible.

Many warm thanks to the numerous students whom I have befriended over the years I have taught. I thank you for the many moments of laughter, hard work, and inspiration you have given to me. Not to mention the puns, of which you guys got the worst. No payment can ever be made for the value of our relationships. You guys know who you are!

And last, but certainly not least, "Tanks Mac!"

Introduction

Clio's Call

Every calling is great when greatly pursued.
Oliver Wendell Holmes, Jr.

I first visited the Gettysburg battlefield when I was ten years old. My father took me there during Thanksgiving break. We stopped at the National Park Service Visitors' Center and hired a licensed battlefield guide to give us the tour of the site. The guide's name was Barbara Schutt and she gave us a marvelous visit. I remember sitting in the passenger seat of our car, hanging on her every word. Much later, when for the first time I took my own students to the battlefield, I hired a licensed battlefield guide; our group was assigned Barbara Schutt! After nineteen years, I still remembered her—and my childhood tour. I kept quiet about the coincidence until the end of the tour—then introduced myself to Barbara and told my students the story. Everyone was dumbfounded! But I think of it this way: All of history, including our own small part in it, is connected; and the people who teach us history can make a lasting difference in our lives.

This book is about making a difference. I hope that reading it will make a difference in your own approach to teaching history as well as in your professional life and the lives of your students. This is also a book about identifying your particular passion in teaching history—and letting that passion lead you and your students on a pilgrimage of learning and sharing—a most rewarding voyage, if undertaken with care, determination, fortitude, and a positive outlook.

On another level, *A Passion for the Past* is about Thomas Jefferson's maxim, "Any nation that expects to be ignorant and free is never what was and what never will be." As a society and culture we need to know about who we are and where we have come from, good or bad, if we are to move forward as a people and a nation through the progress of time. We can't possibly know who we are or where we fit into the scheme of things unless we have a solid understanding of how we have gotten to where we are. It is imperative that we teach our students about who, what, and why we are as a nation. Memory shapes our character. If we do not instill in our future generations the story of our past we may be relegating them to a kind of cultural amnesia. As historian Spiro Kostoff has put it, "What matters in the end is the need to remember."

As long as I can remember, I always loved history. As a youngster I was always asking my parents to take me to visit historic sites, museums, or living history programs. I read history and biography voraciously. As an adolescent and young adult I was fortunate to have two mentors shepherd me along my particular journey. In high school I hooked up with a wonderful history teacher, Neal Adams; watching him in action convinced me that this was to be my calling. I remember in particular a trip he sponsored my senior year to the then Soviet Union. At the time I was enrolled in his Russian Studies course. It was a humanities-based approach to teaching history and we looked at Russian art, read works by Pasternak and Chekov, and listened to music by Russian composers. One point on the trip clearly foretold the kind of teaching I would embrace in my professional life. While visiting Saint Petersburg, we toured the Hermitage (Winter Palace). Standing in the Malachite Room looking out one of the windows, we could see the Neva River and the gunboat *Aurora*, off in the distance. Neal said, "Can you just imagine what it must have been like in 1917, in this room, the night that Lenin launched the October Russian Revolution? Imagine what Alexander Kerensky and the provisional government must have thought looking out this window and seeing the *Aurora* steaming down the river with her guns fixed on their position." I was sold! This was the ultimate learning experience, and I knew then how I wanted to approach teaching history.

In college, during my senior year, I completed my student teaching at an inner-city school in Philadelphia. In a serendipitous moment, I chose to work with veteran teacher Jerome Segal. From Segal I learned that it was within bounds to be outrageous and different in the classroom, provided that you had clear objectives in mind for your students. Segal believed that tapping resources outside of the school building was imperative if your curriculum was to grow and thrive. In addition, he also taught me the art of using all kinds of outside resources—such as newspaper editorials and opinion columns—as effective teaching tools. But, perhaps the greatest gift Segal gave me was the notion that you could have fun teaching. Many of the ideas I use in my classroom came from working with Segal.

In 1980, when I arrived at West Springfield High School in Fairfax County, Virginia, a suburb of Washington, D.C., the prevailing mode of teaching history was the lecture format. Because I was "the new kid in town" that year I fell in lockstep with my colleagues—who was I to make waves? Even though my first year I loaded students down with notes, I felt relatively sure that I was bringing some enthusiasm to telling the history of the United States, but I could tell that a number of my students were still suffering from the "I hate history blues." I knew I had to find a better way.

The summer after my first year of teaching I enrolled in a program offered by the National Archives. Primarily Teaching was designed to provide teachers the means and skills of infusing their history classes with primary source material. This program, still offered today, opened up a new vista for me. I remember on the first day of the course being handed a copy of Richard Nixon's resignation letter. History jumped out at me from that page; and I knew that if I had access to material such as this, it would prove to be a gold mine in the classroom. I also met a number of other, "veteran" teachers from across the country who were seeking the same kinds of avenues in their teaching. As the youngest teacher in the course, I was amazed and inspired by these colleagues, some with more than twenty years experience out trying to improve themselves and their teaching. I soaked in everything they said, asking them what books and authors to read, trying to chart a clear direction for me and my students.

On the first day of school, the following September, I opened my classes by passing out copies of the Nixon letter. It worked! I saw myself mirrored in my students as they held in their hands something tangible from the past. Most importantly, students wanted to know how I had managed to get a hold of a piece of history. They were excited and so was I!

That was 1981. So much has transpired since then. I still continue to struggle, not so much with content as with material. I remember in those early days thinking, "How am I possibly going to fill up fifty minutes of time with something meaningful?" Fifty minutes seemed like an eternity. West Springfield is now on a ninety-minute block schedule, where most of the classes meet every other day, and now my problem is that I have accumulated so much material to teach and share that I run out of time.

Looking back, it would seem then for me that the muse of history, Clio—one of Zeus' nine daughters—has been beckoning me with a siren call. Like those on the voyages of Odysseus, I have answered the call and have let the currents of history bear me into my present and future. Whereas Odysseus sailed in a ship, I drive around in a car with a license plate that reads "Clio Car."

I find teaching very much to be "soul work." I derive a great deal of satisfaction from working with and teaching my students. The classroom is my home and I feel very much that it is where I am supposed to be. Yet, I also feel very much at home at the historic places I visit, either by myself or with my students. At these sites I have discovered a real personal and spiritual connection with the past. Standing there, be it a battlefield or in a historic house museum, I also hear the voices of those who fought, died, or lived at such places calling out, "Teach me."

History is also the study of life, complete with its joys and pains, its mountain-top and valley experiences. At its essence, history is a narrative about people, a most fascinating subject in and of itself. It's the story of who we are, and why we create the things we do: governments, institutions, buildings, bridges, monuments, paintings, and the like. I like to think of teaching history as a way to uncover something about our shared humanity in the narrative of the human experience. The study of history forces us to confront our past, which is sometimes ugly but often can be liberating.

The contemporary history teacher faces the task of trying to make sense of the past for students, as well as the task of helping students develop their own critical-thinking skills. The skills that are taught in history classes are lifetime skills. Students learn how to acquire information, interpret data, and use the acquired knowledge for some type of good. By fostering these critical- or historical-thinking skills in our students, we add life to our democratic traditions, a kind of blood transfusion that is necessary for each generation to have the strength and wisdom to deal with the issues that confront that generation. Studying history is an exercise in thoughtful reflection about the past so as to put the present in greater perspective.

As a history teacher and author, I hope this book instills in you some courage to move beyond the norm in your approach to teaching history and to try some new and different things. I draw inspiration from those people whom I teach about—clearly a nod to those who subscribe to the notion that history is but great biography. Setting an unusual course in my teaching—pun intended—is what I like to refer to as a present of the past, a gift to my students that permits them to recognize their place in the march of time while understanding that those people and events who preceded them affect them to this very day.

In my class, I want my students to "touch" as much history as possible. My students learn in active and dynamic ways. The lessons that I design and implement are meant to be personal so that the students can find their particular connection to the past while constructing their own interpretation of our national experience.

The intent of this work is not to get you to replicate my ideas in your classroom, but to model my objectives as a teacher so that you can tap the genius that lies within you. It will not happen overnight; it will take time to nurture inside yourself the teacher that you want to become. In fact, the process never really stops; I think it's somewhat akin to our democratic history, in that we are always evolving and changing.

At this time all over the country, the spirit of reform in history education is strong and teachers are making a difference for their students, their colleagues, and their profession. There are teachers who are neither creating policy nor playing the politics of education but instead are striving to be their own independent learners, thinkers, and doers, hoping that through the process they can inspire the next generation of Americans. I think that we are collectively making tremendous strides in public and private schools. Ron Briley of Sandia Preparatory School in Albuquerque, New Mexico, has pioneered the use of film to teach history more effectively. Grace Caporino, an English teacher from Carmel High School in Carmel, New York, has taken her students down the path of studying and understanding the Holocaust experience in a more intimate fashion than most teachers by using literature of the period and bringing to life in her classroom the words of the victims and survivors. John Tyler, teacher at the Groton School in Massachusetts, has built a curriculum using a plethora of primary sources to inspire students to think more deeply about the founding of our democratic and political traditions. At Lawrence High School in Lawrence, Kansas, Paul Stuewe instills in his students the need for understanding and valuing the study of the past using strategies such as the Socratic seminar. He hooks his students on history by having them explore and conduct original historical research of their local Kansas history through use of the records housed at the Kansas Historical Society. They also study national historical issues by using relevant documents located at the Truman Library in Independence, Missouri. Linda Miller, a colleague here in Fairfax County, Virginia, has been, since 1979, involved in creating projects and instructional strategies for her students based on the history of the United States Marshal Service. These are but a few of the dedicated history teachers across our country who have discovered the power of authentic teaching by being creative and scholarly in their own right. In doing so they have fostered a natural enthusiasm and love of lifelong learning in those students whose lives they have touched.

Several years ago, I took some students down to Andersonville National Historic Site, in Andersonville, Georgia, to participate in the Memorial Day program of decorating the graves of the Union soldiers interred in the National Cemetery. While there, I met a seventy-three-year-old American ex–prisoner of war. Carl Hedin, a B-17 navigator, had been shot down over France in 1944 and spent fifteen months in a German POW camp. Our conversation was very cordial and Carl was most gracious, sharing with me some of his war stories and memorabilia. Carl asked me if I would read his memoirs, to provide him with a layman's perspective on his work. I was more than happy to oblige. Before we left Andersonville, Carl and I posed together for a picture. Shortly thereafter Carl sent me his memoirs that I read and returned to him with a World War II Fiftieth Anniversary flag, which had been given to me by a local World War II education foundation. Later that summer Carl and his wife, enroute to visit family in New England, stopped in Virginia. I met them for breakfast. As we spoke over coffee, Carl thanked me for the flag. He said that it reminded him of when he was the flag bearer as a member of the Acton Minutemen reenactment company in Acton, Massachusetts. I had lived in Acton, Massachusetts from 1966 to 1970 and was an Acton Minutemen groupie. I attended their events whenever I could and even tried to play the fife for them. It turned out Carl had lived in Acton and marched with the Acton Minutemen for a number of years. We were both delighted and agreed that this was probably why we had struck up a fast friendship. Several weeks later, I was cleaning out a junk drawer when I came upon a package that my Mom had sent me. In the package were a number of black-and-white photographs that I had taken in 1968 with my first camera. They were photographs I had taken at one of the Acton Minutemen reenactments. As I flipped through the pictures, I came across one photograph of a single, solitary figure holding the flag of the minuteman company. It was Carl! In my head I could hear the refrains of Harry Chapin's song "Circle." Several months later I returned to Andersonville for an extended class field trip. Carl agreed to meet our group. While we visited I showed Carl the photograph I had discovered and he identified himself, while the large number of students and their parent chaperones who accompanied me stood in disbelief. I can still hear the chorus of, "No way," and "That's really freaky Mr. Percoco, but so cool!"

As you open the following pages, think about what interests you and how you got turned on to studying about the past. Consider the times you were inspired by someone or some event from history and how you can make that historical moment more meaningful for you and your students. Think about when and where you were when you first made the decision to become a history teacher. As you teach and try to inspire others to study and recognize the importance of history, reflect upon what drew you to the subject. What was it that called out to you? A ghost from the past, such as Lincoln, or King, or a pioneer woman? A historical vignette such as the heroism of Jackie Robinson breaking the color barrier in Major League Baseball or the valor of the Tuskegee Airmen? In answering the call you've embarked on a noble quest. It is my fervent wish that you have an exhilarating journey. Though it can at times be tumultuous, enjoy the ride and reap the numerous rewards along the way. In short, make history.

One

A Present of the Past

Fellow citizens we cannot escape history.

Abraham Lincoln

The school bell rang at 7:30 A.M. on this Monday morning. I completed taking attendance as the groggy members of my eleventh grade U.S. history class fell into chairs. I popped a videotape on Civil War Medicine in the VCR and settled at my desk, composing my thoughts about the questions I would try to plant in my students' minds following the film.

My thoughts were disturbed when Amber, leaning out of her desk whispered to me. "Hey! Mr. Percoco," she began, "Isn't that really cool about your Applied History students out on that archeology dig this past Saturday? Kirsten told me all about it."

My reply was the puzzled expression on my face. It was true my students had just started on their internships and several were working with the Fairfax County Archeology Office, but I knew nothing of what Amber was talking about.

"What are you talking about?" I asked Amber.

"Those Civil War soldiers that they found. You know. The graves," Amber replied. "Kirsten called me Saturday night and told me that her [sic] and the other kids who work for the Archeology Office were out in Centreville helping to dig up some Civil War soldiers that were found in a burial trench."

Thus from a student I first heard about one of the best learning experiences to happen to my students in the six years I had been teaching

1

Applied History, a senior elective for students who have a genuine love of history. Like an archeologist, it would still take some unearthing on my part to learn all the details.

Kirsten, Shannon, Robyn, and Kevin, the four students who were working as interns with the county's archeology office, had—on their first day—made a historical connection impossible to create in a classroom setting. One that will be with them for the rest of their lives.

It turns out that the county had known about the burial trench for a couple of years, but circumstances had forced the archeologists to disinter the bodies that weekend. "We had no choice," Mike Johnson, the county's chief archeologist, told me when I caught up with him on the telephone later in the day. "We had to get the bodies out this Saturday. McDonald's was putting pressure on us because they wanted to get building [on the site]."

I continued to be amazed as I learned each part of the story over the course of what was no longer an ordinary Monday. One of my students brought in a videotape of the TV news report on the dig. My pulse raced as the camera panned the scene. There were my students along with other dirt-covered volunteers standing amidst the cordoned-off area. Then, the camera focused on the soldiers not more than five feet down, some of whom still had boots on their feet and shreds of blue material clinging to their bones. Across a century, my young students were coming face-to-face with America's past.

Finally, two days later, I managed to pull all four students together. They were still excited. Kevin said, "Mr. Percoco, it was awesome! I was touching small bits of rib bones and buttons as I sifted through the screen. It was so cool!"

When I first created the Applied History class in 1991 my ultimate fantasy was to have students, working as interns, be part of a rescue dig of the Civil War soldiers' remains. In 1997, when that fantasy as well as other dreams about this course had become a reality, I felt as if all my work in creating this program had been worth it. History in my classroom was becoming palpable.

What Is Applied History?

What do I mean by the term *Applied History*? It is my approach to teaching not only my U.S. history curriculum, but also a separate senior-level history elective.

During the nearly twenty years I have been teaching, the teaching of history has radically changed, primarily due to the history education reform movement. This movement has expanded the teaching of history to include the *lost* voices of the past, principally those of women and minorities. Additionally, there has been a growing emphasis on using history to teach thinking skills. Consequently, more and more emphasis is being placed on having students learn how to work through the various interpretations of the past while at the same time forming their own historical conclusions. Today, history is more in the public eye than at any time in our past. Americans are responding, at all levels, to an increased awareness of the role of history in shaping our national life. The debate of history has moved beyond the classroom and into the arena of public perception. The citizens of the future, who we teach in our classes, need to be prepared to become engaged in such public discourse if our national traditions and institutions are to survive in the twenty-first century. Hence, it is not uncommon for me to bring into class discussions issues such as the decision by the New Orleans School Board to rename schools that had been named after former slaveholders, including changing the name of George Washington Elementary School. Students frequently read newspaper opinion pieces, which present logical arguments for and against such issues, and bring these to class discussions about a controversy or perhaps the debate over the Enola Gay exhibit. This brings history into their immediate consciousness, in a way that they have never experienced before. History taught in this way gives it an air of immediacy, and provides a solid forum for the exchange of ideas that are so crucial to democracy. As history teachers, we can't be afraid to take on and explore with our students such controversial issues, be they about the place of the Confederate Battle Flag in American life or about a museum exhibit that offers a historical interpretation contrary to prevailing sentiment.

Since my early days as a teacher my style has undergone major transformation. This has been fueled by my desire to make history more meaningful and relevant to the students I teach. I now have more of a hands-on and student-centered focus. It is this hands-on approach that in part describes applied history. Getting students to apply what they learn in class about history in a way that that makes it real and relevant. The course that I teach called Applied History was a natural outgrowth of my growth as a teacher trying to apply history in a meaningful way in the classroom.

I do not consider myself a historian; rather, I prefer to see myself as a history educator. In my approach to teaching history, I fall back on the words of author Nikos Kazantzakis who "suggests that ideal teachers are those who use themselves as bridges over which they invite their students to cross, then having facilitated their crossing, joyfully collapse, encouraging them to create bridges of their own." This is what I see as the heart of good teaching.

Teaching U.S. History

On the first day of school in September, my students arrive at class full of anxiety and anticipation. They are juniors and this year will probably be the most demanding of their high school career. On this day I shake them up. I introduce myself. "Good morning. I am Mr. Percoco and you are in my U.S. History class. Before I get started, I should tell you a few things about myself. I am happily married and have two small children. I want you to know that I am having a love affair. Yes, you heard me right! I said I'm having a love affair."

Stunned silence falls over the room. I can feel the students' eyes following me as I walk up and down the aisles. "She's an older woman—in fact, very old. I have her picture right here in my classroom. That is how much I am in love with her. Her name is Clio, and her picture is over there." I point to a bulletin board on the side wall that I call "Clio's Corner." In the center of the board is a picture of the statue of Clio that sits in the Old House of Representatives Chamber in the U.S. Capitol. Clio sits in her chariot, recording for posterity the record of humanity.

Figure 1–1
Clio's Corner.

I continue with my remarks. Arranged around this photograph are other photographs taken either by students or by me that reflect things we have done, either together or separately, over the years studying history. Some of the pictures are of me at historic sites; some of the images are students posing with a particular Washington, D.C., sculpture they have had to research and write about; while still others are group shots of students on any number of field trips that I have led.

Tell Them You Love History

"Yes, class," I continue, "I love history. And in my class you are going to find that history is anything but boring." Now I have their attention and I tell them that not only do I love history, but I also love my job. I think this may be the first time many students have heard a teacher say this. I see it as very important to teaching. It lets the students know that I am on their side. I proceed to tell the class that I like working with people their age, that I derive a great deal of satisfaction out of it. I begin to tell them where I've been and how my visits to places like historic sites and museums are not only intended for personal growth, but also for finding new things I can bring back to the class to use in teaching. I tell them that this will be unlike any experience that they have ever had in a classroom.

Before I pass out the course syllabus, I brief them on what they are going to learn and how they are going to learn it. I pull the television and VCR to the center of the room and show a clip from the movie *Gettysburg*. In this clip, Colonel Joshua Lawrence Chamberlain of the 20th Maine Regiment talks with some mutinous soldiers about why the country is embroiled in a civil war. It is a very emotional and stirring speech, which deals with concepts such as liberty, freedom, human rights, and other American values. The clip runs less than five minutes but it always hits the mark. This scene from *Gettysburg* helps lay the foundation on which I build my U.S. history curriculum. Here is the text of the speech as found in Michael Shaara's classic Civil War novel, *The Killer Angels*, upon which the movie *Gettysburg* is based. Regardless of the fact that this speech is the fancy of an author's imagination, it still works well in a history class.

> I've been talking with Private Bucklin. He's told me your problem. I don't know what I can do about it. I'll do what I can. I'll look into it as soon as possible. But there's nothing I can do today. We're moving out in a few minutes and we'll be marching all day and we may be in a big fight before nightfall. But as soon as I can I'll do what I can.
>
> I've been ordered to take you men with me. I've been told that if you don't come I can shoot you. Well, you know that I won't do that. Not Maine men. I won't shoot any man who doesn't want this fight. Maybe somebody else will, but I won't. So that's that.

Here's the situation. I've been ordered to take you along and that's what I'm going to do. Under guard if necessary. But you can have your rifles if you want them. The whole Reb army is up the road a ways waiting for us and this is no time for an argument like this. I tell you this: We can sure use you. We're down below half strength and we need you, no doubt about that. But whether you fight or not is up to you. Whether you come along, well, you're coming.

Well I don't want to preach to you. You know who we are and what we're doing here. But if you're going to fight alongside us there's a few things I want you to know.

This regiment was formed last fall, back in Maine. There were a thousand of us then. There's not three hundred of us now. But what's left is choice. Some of us volunteered to fight for the Union. Some came in mainly because we were bored at home and this looked like it might be fun. Some came because we were ashamed not to. Many of us came . . . because it was the right thing to do. All of us have seen men die. Most of us never saw a black man back home. We think on that too. But freedom . . . is not just a word. This is a different kind of army. If you look at history you'll see men fight for pay, or women, or some other kind of loot. They fight for land, or because a king makes them, or because they like killing. But we're here for something new. I don't . . . this hasn't happened much in the history of the world. We're an army going out to set other men free. This is free ground. All the way from here to the Pacific Ocean. No man has to bow. No man born to royalty. Here we judge you by what *you* do, not by what your father was. Here you can be *something*. Here's a place to build a home. It isn't the land—there's always more land. It's the idea that we all have value, you and me, we're worth something more than dirt. I never saw dirt I'd die for, but I'm not asking you to come join us and fight for dirt. What we're all fighting for in the end is each other.

Using this speech helps me to set the tone and content of the course. I focus in on the notion that this nation is, indeed, a remarkable place to live, and that despite the problems we face, the United States still is the one country on earth that many outsiders admire because of our government's guarantees of the concepts of rights and liberty. I tell my students that we are going to examine the United States in all its facets—the good and the bad—because not to do so would be a discredit to them (my students) as well as the true narrative of American history. So every lesson I create—whether it's using public sculpture, playing music, showing a film, or getting students out to historic sites—is plugged into this central idea about our premise as a nation—that we are a model of sorts, still trying to define what is meant by the term, "We the people." My approach for the course is to tell about, and have the students discover for themselves, our story through a narrative format. If you look at the word *history* it is built around the idea of story. Keeping the story at the forefront is tantamount to my process.

Textbooks: Yay or Nay

After I show the film, we discuss Chamberlain's speech and what it means to them. Then I hit my students with my next surprise. I tell my students that I am not going to issue them a textbook, but that I will keep a set of books in the room for in-class use only. You can literally feel the relief flood the room.

My reasons for not using a textbook are as follows:

1. They weigh 5–8 pounds. Why would anyone want to lug something this heavy back and forth from home to school?

2. Textbooks, despite their improvement over the last decade, are still quite boring. Granted they've gotten flashier using better quality pictures and maps, but the writing is stilted. The pleasure of the narrative is lost.

When studying history you need to be able to grasp something tangible and the textbooks don't allow that to happen—most of them have left the story out of history. The study of history requires a spiritual connection with the past, an ability to let your mind go back in time to see, feel, and in some cases taste the eras that were before our time. The way I teach is centered on this extension of the curriculum: getting students to look beyond the textbook and beyond the classroom—out into the world. As I put closure on the first day of class, I point out the window and say, "It's not in here where you're going to do your learning, it's out there."

Granted, not everyone has the luxury or freedom not to use a textbook. If you must continue to use your assigned text, use the examples provided in this book to build your curriculum around your textbook.

The Bradley Commission and Me

Why should you even consider taking this approach to teaching history? To begin with, my style and approach complement the findings of the Bradley Commission for Teaching History in the Schools. In this landmark report, not only was scope and sequence considered important but the active process of learning was considered tantamount to student success and to impart historical knowledge. My approach, particularly in my U.S. history curriculum, mirrors the proposed National Standards for United States History. It is interdisciplinary in nature, focuses on values and traditions of the United States, explores the diversity of the American people and their assorted contributions to our past. It examines those periods in our national memory that are not necessarily of a positive nature, fosters critical- and historical-thinking skills, and puts our history into a contemporary context. In arriving at my goals I don't deviate from the school system's adopted program of studies, a division-wide curriculum project on which I worked. Frameworks are important as they provide a necessary structure, a point of reference, and some direction in which to take students. For new teachers, they are a critical element on the road to good teaching.

I also agree that at the end of the school year, high school juniors who study U.S. history should have retained a certain body of knowledge about this country, values as espoused in the speech by Chamberlain as well as an understanding of the chronology of how these values have been shaped during the American drama.

I expand beyond the framework by putting together lessons that are meaningful and valued by each student. If there is any way in which I play historian, it is in the manner of bringing things that I have learned on the outside into the classroom—be it the paintings of George Caleb Bingham that I link to Jacksonian Democracy or a Civil War medical report, which is tied to the importance of technology in the nineteenth century, or to a vintage song of the 1960s such as Dion's "Abraham, Martin, and John" to highlight the more recent past. It's getting students to construct their own history based on their interpretations. All year long I remind my students that history is subject to interpretation and that we all perceive the same thing from different viewpoints. So it is not uncommon for me to approach a historical topic such as Sherman's March to the Sea by having students read a variety of interpretations using primary sources, such as the diaries of people who experienced Sherman's March, and then reflect on those interpretations to form opinions of their own. So, during the school year I use handouts collected at historic sites, lesson plans developed by the National Archives Education Outreach Office, lesson plans created by the Teaching with Historic Places program, and an array of supplemental paperbacks dealing with various aspects of American history. Students become active learners, engaged in their own learning process.

Part of the work I do to create good lessons often begins with a simple phone call to people who are the experts in an area I want to incorporate into my curriculum. For example, right after I showed the motion picture *Sergeant York* to my classes for the first time, I called his hometown in Tennessee to find out how I could get more information about the real Alvin York. York was the most decorated American soldier of World War I receiving the Congressional Medal of Honor for single-handedly silencing several German machine gun nests and capturing over 130 German infantrymen. When the United States declared war on Germany in 1917, York, who was a member of a small Christian sect from Tennessee, attempted to resist his draft status based on his belief in the teachings of the Bible that killing is wrong. Eventually York chose to fight. After talking with a number of staff members at the local historical society in Tennessee, I was put in touch with York's youngest son who runs his father's

Figure 1–2
Applied History students studying Civil War documents from 1864 of
Andersonville Prison at the National Archives.

home and farm as a historic site for the state of Tennessee. Andy York
gave me all kinds of insights into his father and related stories about how
his famous father had served as a principal advisor to his film biography.
Additionally, he was most interested in what I was doing and how I was
teaching today's students about his "daddy." My students also loved the
story when I told them of my good fortune in talking with him.

Read, Read, Read

In order to teach this way and hone your own teaching skills, you must
read, read, and read history. Keeping up on historical topics and building
new interests will serve you well, particularly if you share them with
your students. There is no better way to teach than by modeling behavior
or academic discipline. Tell your students what you read, and why you
read it, and what you get out of it. Share with students your own discoveries. A writer I really enjoy is Jerry Ellis. His stories about walking the
Cherokee Trail of Tears, retracing the Pony Express route, or walking the
300 miles of Sherman's March to the Sea not only make for great reading, but when they are shared with my students make history more
dynamic and relevant. Here's the story of a man who's part Cherokee,

who decides in 1989 to commune with his past ancestors by retracing their steps. When Ellis' story is put in that context, the students understand the permanence of history. This fits in very nicely with the material I cover on the treatment of Indian tribes in the 1830s and 1840s.

Journal Writing

A technique that I find useful with students is that of journal writing. This freewriting activity is employed when I want students to reflect on a topic or issue. Thoughtful reflection, I believe, is critical to the study of history. Before you can make a value judgment about the past, a component of historical or critical thinking, you have to reflect on it. Journals are used to keep the students focused and to get their ideas down in a concrete form. I also have students share their writings with the class. In sharing, students get to see and hear what other people think and feel about the same subject. Students get to measure their ideas against the ideas of others. Using journals in this fashion also helps me promote the idea of the free exchange of ideas in a respectful manner, thereby serving as a model of the democratic process. It's a very good way to build a sense of community within a classroom. Since journals are one means of assessment I use, I can write or respond to students directly by referring to specific things they write. This allows me to build a personal relationship with the students—an important connection in any teaching. It is also my hope that students will keep their journals, so that in their future they can look back and see where they once were in their past. Using journals effectively will be discussed more fully in Chapter 3.

Test Less

I have increasingly moved away from testing as an exclusive form of assessment. I still do give tests, but less frequently than, say, ten years ago. All of the activities that you will read about in the coming pages are really a hands-on approach to teaching and learning. According to Leo Buscaglia (1982), "Education is from the Latin 'educate' which means to lead, to guide, and that's what it should be." This is precisely how my activities or strategies work—I move away from the position of being the all-knowing teacher to be more of a facilitator of learning. An assignment like my Public History Projects directs students to create a museum display complete with an explanatory brochure. This means that they have to be the ones to communicate the information—they, in effect, become the teachers. Another technique I created is the Historical Head. I use this activity after showing a film, or after having the students read a particular book. In this exercise, students use an outline drawing of a historical figure's head to fill in the brain space with what they believe the person's thoughts and feelings might have been. All of these activities will be described in more detail.

You've probably concluded by now that I am a visual teacher. I also happen to be a visual learner. This became quite apparent to me several years ago, when my wife and I were having a home built. Prior to this I had very little idea of how a house was designed and assembled. But as I watched the stages of construction of our home, I began to understand because I was able to see the process unfold. I believe that this is critical in any form of understanding and mastering a concept, no matter what the concept. So it goes for my students. If I can somehow demonstrate to them a particular historical idea, then they will more clearly understand the topic and its meaning. It's a valuable tool in communicating information.

In many ways I see all of us as both teachers and students. It's a symbiotic relationship. In this atmosphere, U.S. history thrives. It's about real people and real places. It's about the story of America, and how we all fit in and still play a part, and how our nation is always a work in progress—the best kind of work there can be.

Teaching Applied History

One of the things I most enjoy about teaching is that it's a kind of show—my show. In a way that is how the Applied History course got off the ground at my school in Springfield. I was out doing what I like to do second best to teaching, poking around in places in which school teachers are, sadly, never found—archives and museum storage areas. It was 1989 and I had received a summer Fellowship Award for Independent Study in the Humanities funded by the National Endowment for the Humanities and the Council for Basic Education. The purpose of the grant was to afford me six weeks of uninterrupted study of a topic of my choosing—in this case, the life and public sculptures of three prominent American sculptors. My study plan took me up the east coast to observe and analyze principal works of the sculptors, as well as to the museum properties connected to the sculptors, and into various archival holdings. I also was able to meet and talk with experts on the topic. Everywhere I went, I was warmly received and treated like a scholar—a feeling I had never had before. It was a wonderful experience; and not only was I inspired by what I was exposed to, but I also began to think how I could replicate my experience for my students. What would it be like to have kids work with museum professionals and public historians? What kind of similar experiences could be generated for my students so they could have a more active, hands-on approach to the study of history? Out of these ruminations was born the Applied History course. When I first came to the Washington metro area, I remember thinking how much I wanted to be able to take advantage of the rich resources at my fingertips.

Fortuitously, Fairfax County Schools was moving to a seven-period day in the hopes of generating a more diversified elective program. It was the ideal time to launch a new course.

The term *applied history* is very appropriate for this course. It is a class designed for a student who really wants to learn history in a different way and might be toying with studying history in college or pursuing history as a career. The curriculum was set up around first-semester teacher instruction dealing with historiography, archival work, archeology, the methodology of history, historic preservation, and the in-depth reading and writing of historical interpretation and analysis. Field trips were planned for the first semester tied directly to the curriculum and students would read articles in professional journals such as *Historic Preservation* (now called *Preservation*), the magazine of the National Trust for Historic Preservation, and *History News,* the journal of the American Association for State and Local History. Both organizations were only too willing to provide me, free of charge, back issues once they learned of my intent.

That first class seems like eons ago. But the basic structure of the course has not changed since then. As I have grown, and continue to grow as a history educator so, too, has this class; and, as has been the case with my U.S. history class, my teaching and content have also developed further. Now in its eighth year, the class remains one of the more popular electives offered by our social studies department. Since 1991, we have participated in a number of special learning opportunities—what I refer to as academic adventures. We have held telephone conferences with filmmaker Ken Burns, author and historian David McCullough, author and college professor Edward Linenthal, and an unusual telephone conference with a group of high school students in Australia. Guest speakers have included Academy Award–winning film producer Charles Guggenheim; noted Smithsonian historian, Dr. Herman Viola; World War II American ex–prisoners of war; and author/historian Brian Pohanka who served as historical consultant for the motion pictures *Glory* and *Gettysburg,* among others. Each phone conference and special speaker has added a rich dimension to this unique program.

Many of the original internship sites and museum educators and curators still are part of the program today, helping to foster a sense of stewardship for the past among those students under whose direction they work. And with the growth of public history as a profession, the opportunities for my students to work professionally, in history, beyond high school has increased.

Figure 1–3
Applied History students working.

The course has become so popular that each year more students sign up for the course than spaces are available. I have had to put into place a rigorous screening process to insure that the kind of student who takes the class meets the high standards of behavior and expectations that I have established for this special program.

Careers in Applied History

Today more opportunities are available in the history profession than ever before. No longer do you have to be a teacher when you study history. Jobs are available in the private sector as consultants. You can work in a museum or at an archives. At national and state historic sites you can be an interpreter, or participate in living history programs. These are only a few of the many possibilities. Many of the students who have gone through the Applied History course have indeed gone on to careers in history; a number have studied historic preservation at both the undergraduate and graduate level, while others have gone into anthropology and archeology. I have tried to stay in touch with as many alumni as possible, keeping track of their applied history doings.

The Course Outline

Today the course's outline reflects some of the changes that have happened to the study of history in this decade. Let me give you a glimpse of what it was like for those students who were in my class during the 1996–97 school year. This will help you to see how the process unfolds.

In the spring of 1996, ninety seniors signed up to take Applied History. With only one section, enrollment was limited to thirty students. After a two-phase screening process, which involved writing a short essay and an interview, thirty students were notified of their acceptance into the program. Just before school was over in June, a memo went out to these students requesting that they stop by to pick up their required summer readings. These readings included the following: David McCullough's *The Johnstown Flood*, John Hersey's *Hiroshima*, and a packet of readings related to the controversial Enola Gay exhibit at the Smithsonian's National Air and Space Museum. I use McCullough's reading as an example of excellent history writing in the best possible sense of the narrative format. From the outset, I want my students to know how important narrative history is. The other readings are tied to the controversy over the Enola Gay exhibit—the controversial Smithsonian Institution's National Air and Space Museum 50th Anniversary Exhibition related to the Atomic bombing of Hiroshima and Nagasaki that caused a national uproar. This becomes the first case study students will investigate in Applied History. It is important in this class that students see how "messy" the study of history can be. I want them to have to work through a current historical issue: The Enola Gay story is perfect for achieving those ends. After reading *Hiroshima*, the students sort through a packet of articles, assorted op-ed pieces, and letters to the editor that are pertinent to the controversy. All views on the issue are expressed in this packet that not only includes pieces from the *Washington Post*, but also writings from national news magazines, museum journals, and other publications. After they read the book and the packet, students are required to go to the Air and Space Museum to visit and study the exhibit.

During the course of the following summer, after the exhibit opened, I came across the book *History Wars: The Enola Gay and Other Battles for the American Past* edited by Edward Linenthal and Tom Englehardt. This book is a collection of essays about the struggle over the Enola Gay. Linenthal, a college professor who has extensive work in the field of public history, was very much at the forefront of the debate, having served as an advisor to the project. After having read the book, I contacted Linenthal and set up a phone conference between him and my students. Students then wrote essays in which they shared their views on the topic.

Before school starts I send a letter home to all the parents or guardians of the students in Applied History. This letter addresses everything about the class that is important for parents to know. The letter includes the dates and locations of the field trips, a reminder about the summer readings, and a request for parents to get as involved as possible with the various aspects of the program. I end the letter by saying, "Clio and I look forward to working with your son or daughter." Only those students who have had me as their teacher for United States history and are taking Applied History will know who Clio is. They can explain it to their parents. For the other parents and students, it's a device I use to pique their curiosity.

I view parents as critical players in their youngsters' education. This class would not work without their support. Shortly after school begins, I hold an hour-long, evening meeting with the parents to explain in detail the course and its objectives. I ask for volunteer drivers for the field trips and encourage them to participate with the class as fully as possible. I tell the parents that they are more than welcome to participate in any phase of the class they wish. I also suggest that they read the same books the students have been assigned. All of this is another buy-in strategy I use that in this case adds an important dimension to the course.

For the remainder of the first semester the students are engaged in a unit on historical interpretation of history through film, a unit on archeology, as well as writing an extensive research paper on the 1865 trial of Captain Henry Wirz, the Confederate Commander of the notorious Civil War prison at Andersonville, Georgia. We take field trips during the first semester to the National Archives, where students are trained in the use of primary source documents, to Congressional Cemetery, to Gettysburg National Military Park, and to Antietam National Battlefield to participate in the Antietam National Battlefield Memorial Illumination. Additional assignments include two photo essays on historical sites of their choosing and reading several article abstracts from *Preservation* and *The Public Historian*, the journal of the National Council for Public History. All of these activities will be discussed in detail in the following chapters. By the time we are ready to start the second-semester internships, we have become our own tight-knit community.

Right after Thanksgiving, staff members and curators from historic sites, museum properties, and history agencies visit the class to present their particular programs. I do not personally place the students in their internships, but let them choose where they want to work. Internship sites include colonial American homes Gunston Hall and Carlyle House, the Federal Era properties Sully Plantation and the Octagon House, the Smithsonian's National Museum of American History, and the offices and labs of Fairfax County and Alexandria City Archeology, among others. Before being placed, students and their parents sign a contract that indicates the student's learning objectives and work schedule.

By February 1, the internships are up and running. Students are required to work five hours a week at their internship site. The class only meets once a month during the second semester. At that time I collect time sheets and touch base with the students. During the second semester I'm out on the road visiting the students at least twice at each site. The assessment of this part of the program is based on discussions between myself and the sponsoring curator or supervisor and on a self-assessment component provided by the intern.

During this particular year, student-interns did living history presentations, worked on conservation and restoration of photographs and documents, completed extensive lab and field work related to archeology, and organized children's programs at various museums.

In late February, twenty-five of the students and eleven of their parents participated in a field trip to Andersonville National Historic Site for their living history weekend. This was the quintessential applied-history experience putting closure on their research on Andersonville and the trial of Henry Wirz, and bringing together in an exciting and very tangible way all of the components that students had studied and the skills they had developed since the previous September.

The class also has an annual tradition that started at the end of the first year. We hold a year-end celebration banquet that brings together the students, their parents, and the internship supervisors with whom the students work. At this banquet I do a slide show that documents the year's events in Applied History. I also present Certificates of Participation to the students and Certificates of Appreciation to the internship sponsors. A keynote speaker, usually a noted local historian, rounds out the evening. The function gives an exceptional closure for the year. The banquet, always a success, provides me the opportunity to say good-bye and thank-you to everyone involved in the program. It is hard to say good-bye because we have all become so close. I include in my parting comments to the students a quote from President Theodore Roosevelt, who once said, "Far and away the best prize that life offers is the chance to work hard at work worth doing." For me it has certainly come true and it's my fervent wish for my students.

There is no better time to be a history teacher than the present. There is currently more discussion and debate at all levels, on a multitude of issues, regarding the study of history than at any other time. It is incumbent upon us as history educators to seize the moment and guide ourselves and our students over the bridge that Kazantzakis tells us good teachers should build.

Two

Friends and Colleagues
The Art of Networking

Each friend represents a world in us, a world possibly not born until
they arrive, and it is only by this meeting that a new world is born.
Anais Nin

A marvelous painting hangs in the New York Public Library. *Kindred Spirits,* by the American landscape painter Asher B. Durand, is a study of two influential early-American cultural giants, Thomas Cole, one of the Hudson River School painters, and William Cullen Bryant, an influential intellectual. The painting depicts both men standing in the wilds of the Catskill Mountains in upstate New York, admiring the magnificent scenery and sharing their thoughts with each other—a time of personal communion. I like to think of this painting whenever I have an encounter with one of the many people with whom I have built a professional relationship over the course of my years as a teacher. I believe that, just as it is important to build relationships with students, it is equally important to foster good relationships with other adults who are involved with education. This chapter focuses on the importance of building relationships with individuals beyond the immediate environment in which you teach—in other words, outside your classroom as well as beyond the confines of your school district. In the parlance of the age, this is commonly known as networking.

Effective networking not only benefits you, but also your students. It enhances your ability as a teacher, keeping you fresh, and it brings other communities into the classroom, thereby helping students make connections between texts they are reading and the real world beyond the school door. Networking can broaden your horizons as a teacher and instill in you a sense that someone else cares about the work you do, while at the same time reaching out to experts who can offer new ideas or thoughts about your program.

Probably the single greatest device that I have found to help me is the telephone, although e-mail is also making strong inroads on the networking front. In many ways the telephone serves as my bridge to the outside world. In an instant I can talk with my contacts at the National Archives or the National Park Service. I can discuss plans for field trips or projects with museum curators or historic site staff members.

It is important to join at least one professional organization that, by its existence, supports your efforts. I belong to a number of organizations because I have varied interests. However, before you join any professional organization do your homework. Look into the various groups that are part of the landscape of your academic and professional interests. Read their mission statements and philosophies to see if they match yours. Visit their websites, if they are available online. Talk with someone you know who is already a member. I like to be affiliated with groups that can help me refine my teaching, allow me to participate in the dialogue related to history education, and are willing to consider my views in matters concerning the promotion of good history teaching.

The cost of membership and what you receive with a membership should also be taken into consideration. Do you receive a magazine or journal? Who contributes to the professional literature they publish? What professional links can you expect to garner from your membership and participation? I like to be connected with groups that cater to my interests such as the Civil War, public history, and history education. I belong to one group that promotes sculpture and monuments as well as to one of the numerous Civil War organizations. By doing this I am able to keep current on the issues related to history education and satisfy my desire to remain committed to my own particular academic pursuits. In both instances, I continue to grow as a teacher and as an intellectual.

When you network effectively, what you find is that when you open one door it will lead to another door, and another. Just how do these relationships help me—and how might they help you? The best way to present the evidence is to describe my working with a number of outside groups as well as with individuals who are fellow companions in the study of history.

The National Archives

My professional journey beyond the classroom grew out of participation in the Primarily Teaching program, a summer course offered by the Education Staff of the National Archives. This program teaches teachers how to use primary source documents in the classroom by working with vintage documents from the Archives' collection. By the end of the two-week course, teachers create lesson plans based on the documents that they have worked with while conducting original historical research. As a result of my work with the Archives, I was drawn into the circle of individuals in the Education Staff. Wynell Schammel has been head of the Education Staff since 1985. She is a former high school history teacher from Alabama who has taken her creativity into the halls of the Archives. Schammel has a number of duties that bear directly on teachers of all grade levels. Not only does she coordinate the Primarily Teaching program, but she also conducts teacher workshops around the country promoting the use of primary source documents in the classroom. The Education Staff's philosophy is to use facsimile documents, not transcriptions so that students work with the same types of documents that historians are forced to work with—giving them a sense of how a historian must deal with the written record.

Schammel also publishes "Teaching with Documents" articles in *Social Education*, the magazine of the National Council for Social Studies. These article/lesson plans are based on the Primarily Teaching model where a lesson plan is constructed around one focus document—say a Cherokee Nation census record from the 1830s. The articles include appropriate background information to assist teachers in placing the document in its proper historical context. Teachers are free to duplicate the article/lesson plan and the documents for use in their classrooms.

Schammel and her staff also write lesson plans for the Archives website. These lessons can be downloaded for use in the classroom (see Appendix C). In addition, under Schammel's direction, the Education Staff has developed a series of primary source document worksheets that students can use for working with resources like historical photographs, political cartoons, and motion pictures. Most of these materials are provided free to teachers who request them.

The word "outreach," in its best sense, describes Schammel's office. Schammel and her staff are more than willing to assist teachers who are looking for alternatives to using a textbook in their classes.

Over the years I have become close to several of the archivists—those individuals who assist researchers in conducting their research. Rick Blondo, who worked for a time on the Education Staff and is now an archivist at Archives II in College Park, Maryland, has proved to be a valuable ally. When I was conducting my research on Sergeant

Figure 2–1a
Roosevelt/Keneshaw correspondence.

BASEBALL

KENESAW M. LANDIS
COMMISSIONER
LESLIE M. O'CONNOR
SECRETARY-TREASURER

333 NORTH MICHIGAN AVENUE
CHICAGO

Janu 14 1942,

Dear Mr. President:

The time is approaching when, in ordinary conditions, our teams would be heading for spring training camps. However, inasmuch as these are not ordinary times, I venture to ask what you have in mind as to whether professional baseball should continue to operate. Of course my inquiry does not relate at all to individual members of this organization whose status in this emergency is fixed by law operating upon all citizens.

Normally we have, in addition to the sixteen major teams, approximately three hundred and twenty minor teams — members of leagues playing in the United States and Canada.

(Health and strength to you — and whatever else it takes to do this job.

With great respect
very truly yours
Kenesaw M. Landis

The President
Washington,
D.C.

Alvin York in preparation for showing my classes the film *Sergeant York*, Blondo helped me track down a copy of Alvin York's draft card upon which was listed in York's handwriting his objection to military service. Blondo did this by putting me in direct contact with the archival staff at the Southeastern Regional Office of the National Archives

Figure 2–1b
Roosevelt/Keneshaw correspondence *continued.*

January 15, 1942.

My dear Judge:-

      Thank you for yours of January fourteenth. As
you will, of course, realise the final decision about the
baseball season must rest with you and the Baseball Club
owners -- so what I am going to say is solely a personal
and not an official point of view.

      I honestly feel that it would be best for the   ×170
country to keep baseball going. There will be fewer people
unemployed and everybody will work longer hours and harder
than ever before.

      And that means that they ought to have a
chance for recreation and for taking their minds off   ×PP7H6¢
their work even more than before.

      Baseball provides a recreation which does
not last over two hours or two hours and a half, and
which can be got for very little cost. And, incidentally,
I hope that night games can be extended because it gives
an opportunity to the day shift to see a game occasionally.

      As to the players themselves, I know you agree
with me that individual players who are of active military
or naval age should go, without question, into the services.
Even if the actual quality of the teams is lowered by the
greater use of older players, this will not dampen the
popularity of the sport. Of course, if any individual
has some particular aptitude in a trade or profession,
he ought to serve the Government. That, however, is a
matter which I know you can handle with complete justice.

      Here is another way of looking at it -- if
300 teams use 5,000 or 6,000 players, these players are   ×189
a definite recreational asset to at least 20,000,000
of their fellow citizens -- and that in my judgment is
thoroughly worthwhile.

      With every best wish,

      Very sincerely yours,

Hon. Kenesaw M. Landis, ×△
233 North Michigan Avenue,
Chicago,
Illinois.

---

in Atlanta, Georgia, who secured not only a copy of York's draft card
for me, but also other primary source material related to York's eventual service in the military. The copies of these documents, which I
shared with my classes and my colleagues, helped add an extra
dimension to the film.

Schammel and Blondo were also helpful with a lesson plan I wrote for the Organization of American Historians' *Magazine of History*. The lesson plan was based on teaching with documents about the effect of World War II on the wartime status of professional baseball. It all began with my reading Bill Gilbert's book *They Also Served*, which is about professional baseball during the war, where I found out about the 1942 correspondence between Baseball Commissioner Kenesaw Mountain Landis and President Franklin Roosevelt. Landis was eager to know about the President's position on baseball since the war had been declared and was already affecting life in the United States. Roosevelt countered with what has become known as "The Green Light Letter," where he offers his personal opinion that baseball should continue despite the war. One of his strongest reasons for baseball continuing was that it was America's pastime and to give it up for the duration of the war might seriously affect American morale. Roosevelt did affirm his belief that those baseball players who were drafted would in fact be expected to serve their country, which many of them did.

Schammel and Blondo put me in touch with one of the archivists at the Franklin Roosevelt Library in Hyde Park, New York, who secured superb copies of both documents for me. The article was well-received, and each year I look forward to teaching the lesson to my students—who by acclamation every year agree that it's one of the "coolest" lessons we do.

Rick Blondo and I often keep each other informed on topics of interest through e-mail. If something develops that might be of interest, we pass the information right along. By working together with professionals at the National Archives, I have been able to add a rich dimension to my teaching and make history more relevant and meaningful for my students. And so can you.

The National Park Service

The National Park Service can provide you with a wealth of resources. I have been fortunate to work with park rangers as well as staff members at the National Registry of Historic Places, whose office is located in Washington, D.C. I'll describe my interactions with them and where they have led, to let you see what is possible.

It started with a phone call. I had been on a trip to Georgia and picked up a copy of a special issue of *Blue and Gray* magazine that explored the complexities of Andersonville, the infamous Civil War prison. Despite my interest in the Civil War I had never really paid much attention to the story of Civil War prisons. At the time I picked up the copy of *Blue and Gray* I was casting about for some ideas to beef up the Applied History class. My hope was to find a historical issue that had some real depth to it as well as providing multiple interpretations of its particular history. When I started to read the issue on Andersonville bells and whistles went off. BINGO! I had a winner!

After I finished reading the *Blue and Gray* issue, I called the Andersonville National Historic site inquiring if they had any curricular material that could be used by teachers interested in teaching about their site. I knew that several years ago the National Park Service began a program called Parks as Classrooms. This program was designed to help the National Park Service reach into schools. When I contacted the site I was put in touch with park ranger Alan Marsh. He told me about an educational kit that could be sent out, at no cost, to interested teachers. The kit included slides, magazine articles, brochures, a videotape, and one of the first lesson plans drawn up by the National Park Service as part of its Teaching with Historic Places program. The author for this kit just happened to be Marsh. During our conversation Marsh also expressed an interest in helping me create a teaching unit for Applied History.

Emerging from this initial contact was a lesson unit on the 1865 trial of Henry Wirz, the Confederate stockade commander of Andersonville. Wirz was arrested at the conclusion of the Civil War and charged with conspiring to kill the almost 13,000 Union prisoners of war who perished at Andersonville between 1864 and 1865. At his trial, which was held by a military tribunal, Wirz was found guilty of the charges brought against him and executed in November 1865. His execution marks the only time an American has been executed for committing war crimes. This is a complex and complicated story that provided me with a gem of a case for my students to research and argue. For years furious debate has raged between historians as to the guilt or innocence of Wirz. I knew that if I approached the topic with care, as well as with Marsh's help, I could create a wonderful learning opportunity for my class.

In subsequent conversations Marsh pointed me in the direction of material that could be used to help in my research. He suggested books and other evidence I should study. By the following November I launched the case of Henry Wirz, which proved very engaging to students.

Eventually I found my way down to Andersonville. Marsh and the rest of the site staff were more than willing to help me with my on-site research. This led to an invitation to come back to the site for a Memorial Day weekend to participate in the annual placing of the flags on the graves of the Union prisoners who were buried in the National Cemetery. Several years later I took several students, one who's great-great-grandfather had died in 1864 at Andersonville and who was buried in the cemetery, down to Andersonville for the Memorial Day remembrance. It was quite moving as Sean placed a flag on the grave of his ancestor, Stephen Hogan of the 19th Massachusetts, and I felt very satisfied to have been a conduit for his experience. An activity like this could not have happened had it not been for the relationship that Marsh and I had fostered over the years.

Beth Boland directs the program Teaching with Historic Places. Essentially, the National Park Service in conjunction with the National Trust for Historic Preservation has developed lesson plans based around a myriad of American historic sites that are listed on the National Register of Historic Places. These lessons cover the full gamut of United States history including places associated with the rich and famous, as well as the less fortunate, lessons about cultural sites such as the Carnegie Libraries, lessons about the battlefields that dot the American landscape, and lessons that are pertinent to African-American, American Indian, and Hispanic-American history. The lesson plans include primary source material as well as visuals and are augmented with clear and concise teacher-friendly directions. My students, who have worked with these lessons for the past several years, enjoy them. Students have told me that it's like taking a field trip without having to leave the classroom. The Teaching with Historic Places lesson plans can be purchased for a nominal fee from Jackdaws Publishing in Amawalk, New York.

Boland, whose office is in Washington, has been a great resource to work alongside. She's dedicated and enthusiastic about her program and is willing to lend interested teachers any help she can. A historian by training, Boland is very much a part of the community of adjunct professionals who are interested in the work of teachers. In fact, she has made sure that some of the contributors to Teaching with Historic Places are teachers. The training workshops that she has led all around the country have in part produced more than fifty lesson plans that document the diversity of this country very well.

I have been able to assist Boland in her mission not only by writing a lesson plan for the program, but also by field testing and advising her on several of the lesson plans—which are excellent. Our work together led to one of our Applied History classes being featured in a Park Service videotape about the Teaching with Historic Places program. This training videotape was produced to introduce the Teaching with Historic Places program to interested organizations and teachers who want to learn how to use the program in their classes. The film, available through the Park Service, models the use of the Teaching with Historic Places based, in part, on the material that Marsh and I developed about Andersonville. Footage includes classroom application of Marsh's lesson plan as well as a segment of our class field trip to the site.

Part of my philosophy of being a teacher is to be of service, when I can be, to people who serve me by supporting my teaching and thus my students. In many ways schools suffer from being insular institutions. Working with adjunct professionals helps to build communities outside of school. It truly makes a difference in my teaching because it allows for the penultimate teaching experience—sharing a thirst for knowledge and information not only with teenagers, but with other adults who share a similar interest.

Consider contacting not only historical units managed by the National Park Service, but also your state historical societies or preservation offices, usually located in your state capital. Many of these institutions and state museums have now hired curators of education, whose primary tasks are to develop lesson plans and school programs while assisting teachers in building their curriculums.

One-on-One with Private Historians

Effective networking will also connect you with private individuals who share an enthusiasm and passion for history. Kim and Reggie Harris are an African-American couple who have helped me look at U.S. history in a different way—namely music. Professional singers who perform all across the United States, the Harrises have performed and conducted teacher workshops at the Kennedy Center and the National Museum of American History; they have recorded their music on compact disks and cassette tapes. Their albums can be purchased at their workshops or can be found in music stores in the Folk Music section. They tell the story of African-American history through their songs and ballads. They have created several shows, with a keen eye toward education, called Music and the Underground Railroad, a collection of songs and stories relevant to this area of American history. They include traditional Negro spirituals such as "Swing Low Sweet Chariot" and "Free at Last" as well as original compositions like "Heaven Is Less than Fair." Their program, Dream Alive, captures the spirit of the African-American struggle for equal rights. Songs and stories from Dream Alive include works about the Negro Baseball Leagues and about the efforts of all people during the Civil Rights Movement of the 1960s. I always look forward to playing their music in my classes because it adds a dimension to my instruction that I am unable to do on my own. Students respond well to their music for two reasons: They like the sound and they like the message that the songs convey.

However, it is more than the music that has permitted our relationship to develop over the past years; they have been willing to share their views with me on American history, particularly African-American history. Listening to the Harrises, both through their music and in private conversations, allows me to get into the shoes of other people, something that I think is an obligation for history teachers. On several occasions when issues in my classroom have been raised regarding African Americans and their struggles, I have been able to talk through these instances with Kim and Reggie to get a clearer and more balanced perspective on the topic at hand. One year some white students created a videotape project about slavery and unbeknownst to me blackened their faces as part of the program—an activity that some would classify as racist. I don't think they intended to insult anyone, but they did. From the Harrises' perspective I was able to learn a great deal about the reaction that some African Americans have to blackface. Intellectually I knew what that was, but until I had to confront it in my own classroom I really didn't understand it. As a result a set of guidelines were drawn up for teachers and incorporated into our faculty handbooks on how to approach doing living-history projects and videos with our students. These guidelines have proved beneficial for those of us who teach the Humanities.

Much of the material I use about the African-American experience has come through the Harrises. The Harrises' program on the Underground Railroad was based in part upon Charles Blockson's work, an important African-American scholar whose expertise on the Underground Railroad led to his publication of *The Underground Railroad,* a collection of African-American accounts of the abolition movement of the nineteenth century. Once they made me aware of Blockson's book I immediately secured enough copies for my U.S. history students, and students enjoy the selections that I ask them to read because African-American history comes alive through the voices of the participants and becomes quite compelling. The Harrises have also made suggestions on other sources that have proved valuable in my preparation for lessons on Jackie Robinson, Booker T. Washington, Sojourner Truth, and W.E.B. DuBois.

On several occasions, the Harrises have performed at our high school to highly receptive student and faculty audiences. Their dynamic and positive programs include audience participation and leave the audience with plenty of food for thought about what "We the people" really means.

If you are interested in doing more with African-American history in your classroom, I would suggest that you contact the Harrises' agent, whose address and number can be found in Appendix A. You could also contact the History Department at your local community college or university. If individuals in these offices can't personally help you, they will be able to put you in contact with people who can. Many African-American scholars also work with the oral history and folklore tradition alongside curators of education at national and state historic sites that are tied to the African-American experience. Many of these people love to visit schools to perform or work with students. In recent years the National Park Service, state historical agencies, and offices of tourism have put together brochures related to African-American history. These brochures are wonderful resources and are usually free.

Another individual I have enjoyed working with immensely is Dr. Michael Richman, a scholar and the Editor of the Daniel Chester French Papers. As with many of my other connections, this one also started with a phone call. In 1988 I began to dabble with using public sculpture and monuments to teach history. I placed a call to Chesterwood, the home and studio of Daniel Chester French, located in Stockbridge, Massachusetts. French is best known for his monumental portrait statue of Abraham Lincoln inside the *Lincoln Memorial*. The staff at Chesterwood directed me to Richman who lived near me in Takoma Park, Maryland.

When I first called Richman and explained who I was and what I was looking for, he suggested I read *The American Renaissance*, the catalogue for an art show of the same name. I found the book, read it, and called him back. Richman next put me through a phone quiz based on Burke Wilkinson's book on another prominent American sculptor, Augustus Saint-Gaudens. When I had satisfactorily answered all of the questions, he invited me out to his home.

Shortly after I met Richman, I applied for a Council for Basic Education/National Endowment for the Humanities Fellowship Award for Independent Study in the Humanities. I decided to pursue my study of public sculpture and I needed a mentor that would sponsor and work with me. It was only natural to ask Richman. I owe Richman a great deal of credit for the knowledge I now possess on sculpture, which I have incorporated in my teaching as described in Chapter 4. Most importantly he taught me how to look critically at sculpture, training my eye to discern strong works of art from weak ones. After I go on one of my sculpture forays, I always call him and tell him what I have seen. To this day he still drills me on the aesthetic measure of the works I've studied in an effort to keep me sharp.

Since we first met we have collaborated on several projects, most recently a teaching unit on public sculpture for the Organization of American Historians and the National Center for History in the Schools. Additionally, Richman has come to school to speak with my Applied History students about the history of the memorials along the National Mall. He presents a wonderful slide lecture to the students and follows it up the next day with a walking tour of the monuments on the Mall between the *Grant Memorial* at the base of the U.S. Capitol down to the *Lincoln Memorial* at the opposite end. Now we can study all the major monuments in between including the recently dedicated *Franklin Roosevelt Memorial* and *Korean War Veterans Memorial* and the newly installed 1900 plaster version of the *Shaw Memorial* in the National Gallery of Art. And every year Richman puts me on the spot, *in front of my students,* with some question that he expects me to answer correctly. Most of the time I get it right!

Had it not been for Richman I don't think I would have ventured forward with the Applied History class. During my summer of independent

study I was inspired to create the class. As my study came to an end and
with school on the near horizon, I broached the idea of the class to Richman. I had really become excited working with him, other professionals,
and academics. I wanted my students to know the same joy I had experienced. Richman felt that as long as I had the support of the school administration I could make the class a go.

Do Your Own Networking

These are just a few of the many experiences I have had seeing my networking bear fruit. I want to encourage you to meet and make yourself
known to people beyond the immediate world in which you teach. Pick
up the phone. Contact your local historical society and inquire how they
might be able to help you. Or inquire how you might be able to help
them. Scout around your community for people who might be able to
help you infuse your program with a different approach to teaching
about the past. Organizations such as the local Veterans of Foreign Wars
or the American Legion might be able to arrange guest speakers for your
classes. Find out if your local library has a collection of manuscripts that
you and your students might peruse. If you live in a college or university
town, contact the institution's history department and see if there are any
projects on which you can collaborate. Perhaps you can hook up with a
professor who specializes in an area about which you'd like to learn additional information. Start networking and start opening doors. Once you
begin the process you may just find yourself part of a living landscape
painting not unlike Durand's *Kindred Spirits*.

Three

Bumper Stickers and
Other Strategies

I Brake For Historical Markers

Bumper Sticker
Friends of the Pennsylvania State Museum

We may not be able to change the past, but as history teachers we can change the way we teach it. This chapter is designed to help you and your students have fun with history—by creating bumper stickers, heads of historical figures, journals, and photo essays, among other things. Whether you toss out the textbook or adhere to it religiously, you can always be creative by using some of these strategies that also can be seen as tools for authentic assessment. All of these activities are designed to reach the variety of learning styles and multiple intelligences that you will find among your students.

The Academic Bumper Sticker

It started as a spoof on history between my former department chair and myself. We came up with historical puns and made them into bumper stickers. Then I decided to try the game on my students. They loved it. Since then, every one of my regular history classes has ended each quarter by making bumper stickers. Here are the rules:

1. All bumper stickers must be historically accurate.

2. Students must remain faithful to the historical record of the period under discussion, but they may base their bumper stickers on contemporary models.

3. Bumper stickers may not be offensive in nature. They may not contain profanity, nor may they denigrate a person or a group of people.

4. The bumper stickers must be on an 11" × 3" piece of poster board, reflecting the approximate size of real stickers.

5. The students must use color.

Over the years we've made bumper stickers about the American Revolution, the Underground Railroad, the Westward Movement, and the Progressive Era. No matter what time frame you choose to assign your students, plenty of historical information exists from which they are able to draw. They can relate their bumper stickers to the personalities of the period, to themes of the period, or to specific historical events. Some of my favorites over the years have been:

1. John D. Rockefeller Wants *YOU* To Buy Standard Oil . . . Because He Owns All Of It

2. The Great Depression 1929–1940—Eat My Dust! The Next Job's Mine

3. Support The Underground Railroad: The Original Soul Train

4. Manifest Destiny Happens

5. Proud Parents Of A Continental Army Drummer Boy

What do I do with the bumper stickers once they are done? First I evaluate them based on whether or not the students have followed the criteria as outlined on the assignment sheet. Some students are afraid that I will deduct points if they can't draw or aren't artistically talented. I don't. I tell my students this to allay their fears. For those students who have a learning disability or who can't draw or write legibly, I encourage them to work with their resource teacher or to try and use a computer or word processor to assist them with this project. Then I look for an expression of imagination combined with an understanding of the historical relevance of the completed bumper sticker. Of course, evaluation of the bumper sticker is largely subjective—but the important outcome of the project is that students demonstrate what they have learned about history.

Let me tell you a brief story as to how effective this strategy can be in prompting students to learn about the past. Once I had a young lady in class who sat in the back of the room and her body language clearly indi-

Figure 3–1
American Revolution era bumper sticker.

cated that what I was teaching had little interest to her. She would occasionally sleep, never answered questions when called upon, and generally appeared totally disinterested in the course. As part of a large-scale group assignment, she had to cover some aspects of the Spanish-American War; one requirement was to design a bumper sticker related to that conflict. The students were conducting independent research on their assigned topics. On the day I collected the bumper stickers I was absolutely dumbfounded when she turned in hers. The bumper sticker had a spoon, fork, and knife on it offset by a drawing of fried eggs and bacon. The bumper sticker read, "BE LIKE DEWEY. EAT BREAKFAST!" She had in fact gotten it! In her research on the Battle of Manila Bay she had discovered that Admiral George Dewey had pulled his fleet out of the battleline during midbattle to let his sailors eat breakfast. Once breakfast was consumed, Dewey and his squadron went about the business of finishing off the Spanish fleet. I was really impressed by her work. It showed creativity and it was quite intriguing! She had learned something and so had I. I took away from the experience the knowledge that students really can and do learn, provided we as teachers offer activities for people with divergent learning styles.

Once the bumper stickers are turned in for evaluation, I hang them up around the room so that all the students can see what their classmates have created.

Historical Heads

One year, as I was teaching World History, I was looking for a way to make connections between my students and the life of Leonardo da Vinci. I had a film to show about da Vinci and wanted some kind of extended activity to accompany the film. My subject-area administrator suggested, "Why don't you have the students fill in da Vinci's brain?" What a great idea! I went out and got a profile image of the human head from an anatomy book and traced it so that it could be used on a work-sheet and thus was born the Historical Head. This activity, which has been refined in the ensuing years, has proved to be an excellent way to have students get into the mind of historical figures. As a means of assessment it works on a number of different levels: It not only allows students to empathize with a particular character or personality, but that it also permits students to see in a clear and concrete way what knowledge they have acquired. Another advantage is that students like the activity. You can use the Historical Head strategy in a number of ways: with films, outside research, and class readings. In my U.S. history classes, I use the technique several times a year. I've had students complete a Historical Head after watching the film *Frederick Douglass: When the Lion Wrote History*. Students have used it after conducting independent research on Eleanor Roosevelt as well as after reading one of their Civil War choice books.

Creating a Historical Head is simple. You provide students with an activity sheet with the incomplete profile of the head. Direct the students to complete whatever activity you have outlined for them, be it watching a film or reading a book. After they have finished their primary task, they are to fill in the head with the ideas, thoughts, visions, and motivations of the person on whom they are working. I usually have students create at least five images that they draw inside the head outline, or in the case of students who are not too sure about their artistic ability, they cut and paste images from magazines or downloaded from the Internet into the brain space. Students are to number each image and on the back of the sheet write a corresponding statement about that image and how it is tied to that particular person. In cases where they are required to do independent research, they have to document on the back of the page where they found their information. I encourage the students to use color and imagination in their final product. I evaluate Historical Heads by making sure that the information is correct; I also look for back-up details in the explanatory statements that correspond to the images.

One of the things I most enjoy about using the Historical Head is that it is so adaptable to any person or time period. In fact, not all of my Historical Heads are related to a specific personality. I sometimes have students create them based on a particular group of people, say, immigrants from Southern Europe at the turn of the century, or individuals who have escaped on the Underground Railroad or assisted runaway slaves. The choice is up to you because the template is so generic.

Historical Heads force students to put themselves into the shoes of another person. Completing this activity, students become more aware of the emotional facets of history. For example, you could use this technique by having students read the letters of a particular individual or set of individuals, such as the letters between John and Abigail Adams. Not only do

Figure 3–2
Historical Head.

Name *Nick Welikozkiy*   *US History*
                                                  Mr. Percoco

Historical Head #3

Frederick Douglass: When The Lion Wrote History

Directions: Please fill in the cranial space below with the thoughts, ideas, visions, and motivations
             of Frederick Douglass. Please use a minimum of four images and be sure to number
             them on the back with a corresponding statement that identifies each image. Again, use
             color and tour imagination to complete this activity.

This activity is worth two grades.

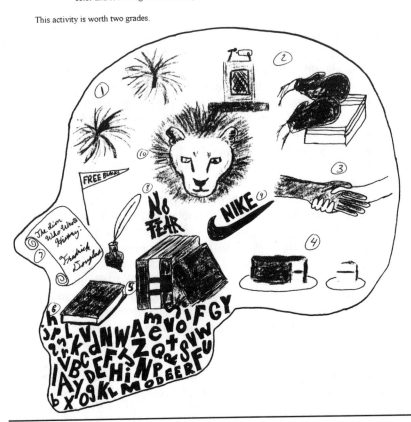

students have to read the letters, but by completing a Historical Head
based on their understanding of the letters students are able to make a
much more concrete link to that person or persons. They have to translate the words into pictures, which at some level brings the experience of
the person on whom they are working much closer to home. Students

can then compare their own life's experiences against the life of the person whose Historical Head they must complete and the person becomes real in a much more dramatic way.

Using Journals

Having students write journals as part of creating student portfolios or for other means of student assessment has been popular for a number of years. Early in my teaching I used journals, somewhat ineffectively, I thought, assigning questions rather randomly with no particular rhyme or reason. I was attracted to the idea of having students write in a free-association manner, but I now see I needed to give more concrete direction for students to focus their writings. I wanted to have students write about their ideas, thoughts, and feelings, based on some kind of historical reality that would permit them to explore their own independent views of history—independent from mine. Then I attended an inservice program led by Dr. Henry Steffens, History Professor at the University of Vermont, who is regarded as an expert in using the journal technique to have students discover the value of writing about history. Steffens' work has appeared in *The History Teacher, The Organization of American Historians Council of Chairs Newsletter,* and in the *Journal Book* edited by Toby Fulwiler. After listening to and watching Steffens model his technique for those of us who attended his session, I began following his lead in getting students "Writing to Learn History" through active journal writings. According to Steffens, "giving history students the opportunity to do more informal and expressive forms of writing, free from immediate evaluation, will help them to learn history better. Informal, expressive loosely structured writing allows for the exploration of ideas, for speculations, for the considerations of implications, for the development of ideas in stages of increasing complexity, and for the recall of information from previous experience. Through more expressive, informal writing, students have an opportunity to develop ideas, to 'see' those ideas for the first time, and to decide whether they agree or disagree with them . . ."

Based on Steffens' writings I put together a handout, calling it "Writing to Learn History—The Journal Process." The handouts mirror the idea that these expressive writings are designed to get students to open themselves up to different possibilities of learning about history. It is my hope that they record their ideas and thoughts in a way that helps them emerge as independent thinkers. I urge students to plan on keeping their journals well after they have finished with my class so that in years hence they can look back at their journals and see what they once thought about a particular topic. Journals are also good for prompting class discussions.

All of my students are required to purchase an inexpensive marble, bound composition notebook, which for the most part is kept in the classroom. Whether it's for homework or writing in class, I ask students to write for about eight to ten minutes on a particular question, with the intent of filling up the entire side of one page. Journal questions are most often based on films we have watched, activities that have a hands-on application, guest speakers they have listened to, field trip evaluations, slide images that have been shown, or readings. In anonymous course evaluations that my students complete for me at the end of the year, they have indicated that by writing journals they were able to watch their learning unfold, particularly since journals were tied to areas that allowed for latitude in interpretation.

Over the course of my yearlong U.S. History class, students write in the neighborhood of forty journal entries—roughly ten per quarter. About half that number are given for the classroom semester of Applied History. One journal assignment I give is called "Bridges." I use this assignment at the beginning of the year, when I am trying to get students to understand the notion of the study of history as being a bridge to understanding the past. We watch Ken Burns' film, *Brooklyn Bridge*. After watching the film, I put up slide images of bridges I have photographed around the country. Some of the bridges are covered bridges in Vermont and New Hampshire, while others cross the Mississippi and Missouri rivers; still others are great urban bridges, such as the Golden Gate Bridge in San Francisco and the George Washington Bridge in New York and New Jersey.

Next, I tell a personal story about my freshman year at Temple University. That year I often got homesick. When this happened, I climbed to the laundry room in my dormitory, which was at the top of the building. There I gazed out the window at the Benjamin Franklin Bridge, which crossed from Philadelphia to Camden, New Jersey. By doing this I could connect with my friends and family in New York because I knew that crossing that bridge meant I was on the road to home. By telling this story, I reach students in a personal way. If they know that I'm willing to share some of my life's experiences with them, then perhaps they'll do the same with me. It is at this point that I direct students to their journals. I ask them to write about some bridges that they've crossed in their lives. These bridges can be either real, having taken them to another physical place, or symbolic, having taken them from one point in their life to another. Either way they choose to write their journal assignment, I have still taken them back into their particular and personal past, so it still remains a bridge to some sort of history.

The responses of the students are wide ranging. Some would rather talk about being on a real bridge and how this to them was a symbol of being close to a grandparent or a friend's house. Others talk about bridges that they have actually walked across, such as the Golden Gate or Chesapeake Bay Bridge. They reminisce about how they felt being suspended over a particular body of water and how at first it seemed frightening, but after a while it became more comfortable. Some students have crossed the Brooklyn Bridge itself and can relate to the film and assignment on a different level. Often they write about something in the film that struck a chord in them. Then there are those students who take a greater personal risk and talk about some episode in their lives, be it their parents' divorce, the death of a loved one, a serious illness, even the loss of a pet or an argument with a friend. No matter how they choose to respond, reading this particular journal entry helps me cross that often tenuous and undefined bridge that exists between student and teacher.

I evaluate journals based upon the depth of thinking that is demonstrated in the students' responses. While I encourage them to write a full page, I know that for some students this is not possible. As long as they show me that they are involved with answering the question, with some depth, the journal entry will pass my inspection.

Journals work for both me and my students. They promote good thinking skills and provide students a different kind of outlet for their learning. Students enjoy writing them because they know that their answers can't be wrong. I would think that as a student that would make all the difference in the world. They help me to understand my students better and permit me to see into their minds, something that I might not be able to glimpse through expository writing. I encourage you to try out the technique and discover with your students what bridges you can cross together.

Supplemental Readings and Their Application

I rely on a whole assortment of extended reading material to teach history. Teaching history in this way permits me to provide students with a greater latitude of choice in specific readings, while at the same time giving them a sense of the big picture of history. The materials that I have picked are based on my particular interests and from time to time allow me to move back and forth across different historical themes. Again, you can make your own choices as to what material you use.

I start my U.S. history course with an introductory unit in which students read *Milestones into Headstones: Mini Biographies of Fifty Fascinating Americans Buried in Washington, D.C.* by Peter Exton and Dorsey Kleitz. The book includes biographies of such luminaries as F. Scott Fitzgerald, Medgar Evers, Omar Bradley, Adelaide Johnson, and Joe Louis. When I introduce the book I inform students that there is going to be a multiformat assessment of their reading. First we will have an objective test, then students will write an essay based on a quote from Oliver Wendell Holmes Jr., "Every calling is great when greatly pursued," which is found on the opening page of the book. Students also will pick one person from the book and complete a Historical Head about the person, and finally students are to pick one person from the book who inspired them and visit that person's grave. While at the grave site students are to have two photographs of themselves taken at the grave. One picture will be posted at Clio's Corner and the other photograph will illustrate a journal entry they write about making their pilgrimage to this particular person's grave. In order to make students more comfortable with their grave site visit, I remind them that many people visit the graves of noteworthy Americans all the time. Then I model for them, using slides, my personal visits to graves of famous Americans including poet Robert Frost, Eleanor and Franklin Roosevelt, and a slide of me standing next to the grave of General George Henry Thomas, a hero of mine from the Civil War. It should be noted that students do not have to do their Historical Head based on the person whose grave they have visited. If they choose to do so that is fine, but I desire to provide them with some latitude by not restricting their interest entirely to one individual. The multiformat assessment also provides me with an opportunity to reach all types of learners and measure what they have learned through a variety of formats. I also think that by not restricting the evaluative technique solely to tests, students are exposed to a very active kind of learning.

I have discovered by using this book and then following through with the various assignments that it works on several different levels. Students get to make several choices; I have found that they like that option in the classroom. Because they can choose a person, they get to make a much more personal connection to that individual. In their choosing the various individuals, particularly for the Historical Head activity and the grave site visit, I get a better understanding of that particular student. Not surprisingly, students select individuals based on mutual interest. For example, students who are in the school band often opt to visit the grave of John Philip Sousa in Congressional Cemetery, while those who are interested in politics often visit the graves of John F. Kennedy or Robert F. Kennedy in Arlington National Cemetery. The grave of F. Scott Fitzgerald and his wife Zelda in Saint Mary's churchyard in Rockville, Maryland, is also a popular choice among students as is the grave of Henry Adams and his wife Marion, located in Washington's Rock Creek Cemetery, adorned with an enigmatic sculpture by Augustus Saint-Gaudens. In their journals, students often write that they thought this was a good assignment because it made them aware of the world that exists nearby them while at the same time they realized that the people whom they had read about in *Milestones into Headstones* were in fact real, live, breathing human beings. Parents have also told me that they thought the activity was creative as well as productive, indicating that they wish their high school history teacher of ages ago had created similar activities.

I use a similar format when teaching about the Civil War. I have selected a number of titles, drawing from first-person accounts based on actual experiences during the Civil War. The individuals chosen also reflect a diversity of people and their experiences of that tragic conflict of mid-nineteenth century America. The books are usually memoirs, diaries, or collections of letters from that person. The books include accounts of men and women, blacks and whites, and Union and Confederate soldiers. Again, students are able to make a choice based on their particular interest or background. The particular books I use are *Fallen Soldier: Memoir of a Civil War Casualty* by Andrew Roy, an excellent account of a Union soldier's road to recovery from a severe wound; *On the Altar of Freedom: A Black Soldier's Civil War Letters from the Front* by James Henry Gooding; *Co. Aytch* by Sam Watkins, a Confederate soldier from Tennessee; *The Journal of Charlotte Forten* that tells of being raised in an African American abolitionist family and life as an African-American woman during Civil War America; and *A Southern Women's Story* by Phoebe Yates Pember, which is her account of serving as a nurse in wartime Richmond, Virginia. Certainly there are many other titles to draw from, but I have chosen these because they are not too long nor difficult for students to read and they provide a very personal glimpse into the life of an American living at the time.

After the students read their Civil War choice book, they complete a Historical Head and a journal entry. In addition, since not all of the students in the class are reading the same book, I break the students into groups based on titles and ask each group to come up with a list of seven or eight points from the book that their classmates should know about. As a group they are to write these points down on newsprint and share them with the other students in an oral presentation. All of the students are responsible for getting information about each book into their notes; as part of their evaluation, they will be tested on material from all of the books. By doing this I ensure that all of the students in the class get some degree of exposure to all the materials.

Another book that I have had success with in the classroom is David Halberstam's *Summer of 49*. This is a wonderful social history of the United States seen through the lens of baseball. When I first read *Summer of 49* I was intrigued by how much this book touched on the fabric of post-World War II America. The issues of ethnicity, race, and life in the United States seemed to leap right off the pages all against the backdrop of baseball. It is very easy to make connections between this book and previous material that we have covered on immigration. Names like DiMaggio and Berra, Pesky and Kiner read like a *Who's Who* of immigrants. And the place of Jackie Robinson is also crucial in setting the scene of America in 1949. What I have had students do with reading this particular book is write an essay based on how the book reflects life in America at the time. Students also are to examine the difference between athletes at mid-century America and athletes today. This focus is usually explored through journal entries. It's my sense in reading their journals and essays that students today realize how much they have missed out on a very special time in American social and sports history.

When selecting book choices be certain to choose books that you are comfortable with and feel as if you can teach. Look for books that have some sort of hook to them that will make students want to read them. And always, no matter what you read of a historical nature, think about how you might utilize it in your classroom with an eye toward how this particular book served to inspire you.

Creating Photo Essays

I've always been attracted to books that convey their message through photographs rather than exclusively through the written word. There's something powerful in a story that a photograph tells. In an effort to get my students to appreciate the history in their environs I decided to create a project activity to go beyond the *Milestones into Headstones* assignment. I wanted students to immerse themselves in a particular space related to a specific time period. So I decided to try having them create photo essays. I have used this assignment strategy in both my U.S. History and Applied History classes. The photo essay has proven to be a very successful teaching and learning device. Students and parents sometimes make a family outing to a particular site. In other cases parents let their sons or daughters, who have obtained their drivers' licenses, make the trip on their own.

The outline and format of the photo essay is very simple. Students choose a historic site, visit that site, and then document their visit through photographs, which they then arrange creatively on a poster board. The site's name must be part of a title arrangement, and all of the photographs are to be appropriately captioned. Students may opt to complete this activity in small groups of two to five, or they may choose to work alone. I encourage students to use brochures, or any other printed material from the site, to help tell the story of their particular visit. In addition, I ask students to appear in at least one of the photographs as part of their exhibit.

After students have completed their photo essays, they present them to the class, discussing with their classmates the particulars of each site and the merit of their visit. We then hang the photo essays up around the

Figure 3–3
Students presenting a photo essay.

room for everyone to enjoy. I also like to share the photo essays I have created with students. Some of the places I have chosen include Johnstown, Pennsylvania; Harry Truman's Independence, Missouri; and the Baseball Hall of Fame and Museum in Cooperstown, New York.

In my U.S. History class, I assign the photo essay when we are studying the Civil War and provide students with a list of sites within reasonable driving time from Springfield. I make available a large collection of brochures and literature that I have collected. This helps them decide where they want to visit. I advise the students to first stop in at the site's visitor center and take advantage of any orientation that the site might offer. Part of my objective is to get them into a frame of mind where they will learn as much as they can from their visit, taking away more than just photographs. I want them to get in touch with the past in a way that perhaps they haven't done before. I suggest that they read something about the site before they take their trip. I am often pleasantly surprised when students come to class with their photo essays, depicting a range of the Civil War sites in the northern Virginia area. Some students have gone as far as Appomattox Court House, the site of Robert E. Lee's surrender to Ulysses S. Grant, a four-hour drive from Springfield. Other students have looked into when there will be Civil War living history programs and documented a visit that has a whole different element. Students have also gone to the state Capital, Richmond, photographing images from that city that are related to the war.

The Applied History students have a bit more latitude with their site choices. They can document any historic site they choose. Consequently I have had photo essays turned in from all over the United States, as students visit places during school holidays. One year I had a student document the small town from Maine where his family had roots for over a century. In fact, the family graveyard, which was documented in the photo essay, is still active and this student intends to be buried there. As part of his photo essay, he included copies of archival photographs from his family tree to help tell his story. Another student did a photo essay on another Springfield—this one in Kentucky—where Zachary Taylor's home and grave are located. Some students have gone to the Maryland Renaissance Festival, which provides another take on living history by presenting a full-fledged festival related to the late Middle Ages or early Renaissance periods in Europe. Many states now sponsor annual Renaissance festivals that bring to life the music, art, theatre, and daily life of the era. I have learned that the possibilities are endless. It also gratifies me that students are willing to go beyond the norm and extend themselves.

Again, I sometimes follow up the assignment with a journal entry assignment to get the students to put into words accounts of their visits. You can certainly duplicate this activity in your classroom. History is everywhere, and getting students to explore and experience history in this fashion will take them far into learning about what happened at a particular time and place. You'll be surprised with the stories that come back into your classroom as the students try to top each other with tales of their particular journey.

Using Music

Music often can be used to teach history. Consider the narrative history songs, such as Johnny Horton's "The Battle of New Orleans" or period music such as music from the Jazz Age or the protest music of the 1960s and the Vietnam Era. There are also thematic songs and songs about America and our place in history. I have used all kinds of music to teach about the past. At the beginning of the year in my U.S. History class, I play several songs about America and ask students to select one of the songs that best represents their view of the United States. The songs include "America: The Dream Goes On," a patriotic orchestra and choral piece; "Black Man," a song written and performed by Stevie Wonder for the American Bicentennial; Bruce Springsteen's rock ballad "Born in the USA"; Paul Simon's and Art Garfunkel's "America"; and Lee Greenwood's "God Bless the USA." After listening to the songs the students talk about their reactions to each song, and we hold a class discussion on why different songs can mean different things to different people.

I also like to use classical music in my classes, so the tunes of Gershwin and Copland can often be heard coming from my classroom. One of the more interesting activities we've done involved combining the Historical Head with Anton Dvorak's Ninth Symphony, *From the New World*. Dvorak was not born in the United States, nor was he an American citizen. He came here in the 1890s from Czechoslovakia, to teach music for a short period in New York City. While he was here, he traveled around the country, making all kinds of observations about America and Americans. Being a kind of musical de Tocqueville, he put his thoughts to music and in 1894 *From the New World* was first performed. After I tell students a little about Dvorak, I ask them to interpret Dvorak's work by making a Historical Head. This lesson is taught in my U.S. History class when we are talking about American history at the turn of the nineteenth and twentieth centuries. I explain to students that this piece was a celebration of America up to that time in history, and that Dvorak was interpreting our history and progress as a nation through music. The task of the students is to fill in the Historical Head based on how they interpret the music and how they see American history up to that time. Again it works on a number of different levels, tapping all kinds of learning and thinking skills while allowing me to use the Historical Head for different lessons.

At the end of the school year I also like to use a little known song by Harry Chapin, "She Is Always Seventeen." This song was also written for the Bicentennial, and the lyrics, which I found on the Internet at a Harry Chapin website and provide to the students, covers American history from the election of John F. Kennedy until 1976. It's a great song with great lyrics that can be woven into your class. I break the lyrics into segments and assign different students different segments. After we listen to the song, they have a week to research their particular lyric stanza and then report back to the class. Before students report I play the song one more time. There are clues within the context of the lyrics that can assist them as they work through the song. One of the sources that I suggest they use for their research is talking with their parents—a kind of oral history source—as many of their parents were growing up in the United States at the time about which Chapin writes.

Once we have pulled together the lyrics and their historical references, I ask the students in their journals to discuss the meaning of the song's title, "She Is Always Seventeen." While I have my own thoughts about its meaning, I don't share them with the students until after they have reported to the class. A number of students decided that the song meant something about American youth. One student wrote, "I'm going to say that 'she' is the youth, the youth of America that never grows old. Only the individuals change. I mean everyone always says that our future lies in our children. When you're seventeen, you don't care about anything other than what you believe in. Youth is not jaded by personal failures." Another student wrote, "'She' seems to be like a girlfriend or a female companion with whom Chapin does all of these things, yet 'she' is more than that 'she' is also a representation of the American spirit, perhaps even Lady Liberty. 'She' is always seventeen because she represents the optimism of the American youth in the time period. 'She' shares her sorrow because of some of the more painful aspects of American history. 'She' shows hope and promise because 'she' continues to stand up and fight for a better country and a brighter future. 'She' pickets, 'she' protests, 'she' makes statements, thus 'she' makes a step toward the betterment of our society." A third student said, "I think the title reflects the whole movement of the sixties and seventies. No matter what it was, civil rights, antiwar, or women's rights, a great deal of the movement was youth. They sparked it and their energy fueled it. When you're younger, optimism is at its peak and so they're willing to try and change things. Chapin's saying there will always be a movement because cynics may quit but there will always be a new generation of seventeen-year-olds ready and willing. They are a necessary part of revolution because they have no fear of dramatic action and they speed things along with their natural impatience." Personally, I see the significance of seventeen as referring to the year 1776 connecting with 1976. But I also agree with the students who assess the song's meaning as being tied to American youth. I remind my students that this song was written for the Bicentennial and that's how I made the connection with the number seventeen.

A Public History Project

An interesting class project emerged as the result of my membership in the National Council on Public History and the National Council for History Education. I think most teachers who teach a survey course of U.S. history wrestle with the same dilemma every year—how to find a balance in covering the entire spectrum of American history with content that has depth. Until recently this proved to be one of my toughest challenges. I was also trying to figure out how to make museum learning and the concept of public history a reality in my class. My students know how much I try to bring the outside world into the classroom, so they were game for what I proposed. On a handout for the students I defined the idea of public history—history that is presented in a public arena, such as a museum, a historic site, a traveling exhibit so that it is a kind of historical interpretation that is very much a part of the public eye and public policy creation. We talked about this definition and then I laid out my plan. Students would be broken into groups of no more than five and assigned a time frame between 1870 and 1930. Based on their time frame they would design and create a museum exhibit. For the time frames I turned to the Fairfax County Public Schools United States History Program of Studies (POS) and NCHE's (National Council for History Education) guide for teachers, *Building a United States History Curriculum*.

The Program of Study was recently revised to reflect the changes that have been made in the arena of history education reform. The new POS breaks down time periods into "content questions." For example, for post–Civil War America, roughly 1865 to 1900, one of the content questions is, "In what ways did changing patterns of immigration to the United States and the movement of people within the country create new social patterns and conflicts?" These content questions, based in part on the National Standards for United States history were created by a committee of teachers (of which I was a member) from the school division. They were designed to provide teachers clearer guidelines for what history is to be presented to students. While it outlines what needs to be taught, it leaves how it will be taught to the individual genius of each teacher.

I then merged the Program of Study with the specific points for the chosen time frame based on the bulleted concepts as outlined in *Building a United States History Curriculum*. *Building a United States History Curriculum* is very topic specific and was helpful in getting students to focus their projects. The marriage of these items worked very well as shown below:

Immigration, Migration, and City Life in America

- Millions move from farm to city between the Civil War and World War I; over 25 million immigrants arrive; southern blacks begin migration to northern and midwestern cities.

- Growth of urban-ethnic neighborhoods, institutions, trades, occupations; e.g., Chinatown and Little Italy.

- Resurgence of nativism against hyphenated Americans; controls and restrictions on immigration; Chinese Exclusion Act, 1882.

- Urban population soars: the great cities (e.g., New York, Chicago) and hundreds of smaller cities (e.g., Bridgeport, Toledo); by 1920 census, the majority of Americans live in urban centers.

- Attractions of city life: lights, water, sewers; schools, libraries, museums; dance halls, concert halls, theaters.

- The underside: noise, crime, pollution, poverty, squalor (Jacob Riis photos); racial and ethnic conflicts; start of flight to "streetcar suburbs."

- The need for services and defenders; the rise and workings of ethnic political bosses and machines; Tammany Hall.

Project Description

For this assignment students are to act as a collective of history museum curators who are to design a museum exhibit and then present their chosen Content Question and Exhibit to the class. The exhibit will be in a multimedia format—something that will engage all of the senses. Students should consider visiting a local museum to see how exhibits are presented to the public.

Requirements

Each group will:

- Design and create a three-dimensional exhibit that incorporates photographs, images, graphs, maps, charts, primary source documents, and artifacts with appropriate captions. Consider also creating some sort of interactive display that engages the visitor physically as well as spiritually with the past.
- Design and create a brochure that explains and accompanies the exhibit.
- Give a twenty- to thirty-minute oral presentation that provides an explanation of the exhibit; this may include using music, video clips (you may create one yourself or use a commercially produced one, provided I preview it), slides, a living history program, and so on. The presentation must be set in proper historical context and cover the range of time presented in the Content Question.
- Turn in a group bibliography that follows the school style manual (based on the MLA format), with no fewer than seven sources.

The exhibit and presentation should include, relative to the chosen time frame and Content Question:

- images of important personalities,
- important events,
- cultural, social, economic, and poltical implications and impacts,
- five primary source documents, with an explanation of their pertinence to the topic,
- a handout for classmates with a list of at least seven important facts, ideas, or concepts related to the topic.

The Finished Product

Students are given eight weeks to work on this project before it is due for presentation and evaluation. We spend some time in the school library researching the various aspects of history as outlined by the Content Questions. I set aside approximately four, ninety-minute class periods for the students to present their projects in chronological order. My evaluation is based on how well the students have followed the guidelines, the depth of their research as evidenced by their exhibit, presentation, and bibliography, and how clearly they have demonstated their understanding of their Content Question. While one group is presenting, the other students in the class take notes. In effect the students become the teachers of the material. Students enjoy working on this project because it allows them to do in-depth research in a hands-on fashion. The project also prompts students to think about what information is important for their peers to know. It makes them responsible for not only learning the material but also presenting it in a coherent fashion. This project has an interdisciplinary component and asks students to consider the big picture of history while at the same time asking them to determine the important incidentals of a time period. Finally, the project embraces the notion of reaching divergent thinkers, students with different learning styles, and engages multiple intelligences.

Any of the aforementioned strategies or lessons can be incorporated into your program. They are easy to construct, very student centered, and lively. My students have enjoyed them as a means of learning, hearing, and seeing about the past. The students know from their active participation in these activities that history has many facets and is multidimensional. History becomes more than just dates in a book that they have to be forced to digest and then spit out for teacher on test day. I think that they are lessons that will last a lifetime. It sure would be nice some day to see a bumper sticker on a car that reads, "If you can remember the past, thank your history teacher."

Four

If Statues Could Talk
Using Monuments to Teach

You can do anything you please, it's the way it's done that makes a difference.
                    Augustus Saint-Gaudens, American Sculptor

His estate sits back about a mile from the main road, New Hampshire Route 12. The approach is a curvy lane typical of northern New England roads that are removed from the main town area. The road is lined with majestic oaks and pines, forming a kind of canopy leading to the visitors' parking area. The main house, at first glance, looks like any New England Federal-style house: It's symmetrical, with a verandah, large windows, and an inviting front entrance. This is the estate of the late Augustus Saint-Gaudens, perhaps the most celebrated American sculptor of the late nineteenth century—the creator of such works as the *Farragut Memorial*, the *Shaw Memorial*, and the *Adams Memorial*. The home, called Aspet— along with surrounding outbuildings, including his studio—is now the Saint-Gaudens National Historic Site. It was here that Saint-Gaudens transformed so many of his ideas into monumental works of public sculpture reflecting the values and attitudes of many Americans during the years between the Civil War and World War I. And it is here that, whenever I visit, I find my spirit renewed and energized for another year of teaching.

I first came here, to Cornish, in 1988. The visit marked a transition in my teaching style, leading me down a road in my personal and classroom education practice that I still travel. At the time I remember thinking how wonderful it was to be at the home of this master American sculptor whose works had found their way into my teaching and had allowed me to make history more meaningful and vibrant for my students.

Saint-Gaudens National Historic Site has a kind of special hold on me that I think allows me to create magic in the classroom. This magic I have tried to share beyond the four walls of my classroom by writing a number of articles on my use of Saint-Gaudens and his artwork in my class. I have also built over the years a bond with the staff members of the site who have encouraged my continual writing and teaching about Saint-Gaudens. Writing to share with a larger audience, including you, is an important part of what I see as my role as an educator. By doing this I also validate the mission of the site, thus giving a prime example of teachers and public historians working together.

At the site, I can "see" and "feel" the people of the Cornish Art Colony, those artists who followed "Gus" here and developed a colony at the foot of the master's domain. I can let my mind's eye wander and catch a glimpse of the Masque of the Golden Bowl, the tribute organized by the Cornish Art Colony, that was held on these grounds in 1905 to honor the sculptor and his life as he struggled with cancer. Walking down beyond the main property, I follow the trail that leads to the grave site of this American icon, who for me has become a model to emulate in good, solid teaching.

The Statue-Student Connection

I've discovered that sculpture can help in many ways to tell our story—the story of the United States. It's the allegorical and monumental nature of commemorative sculpture that makes it so attractive for use in the classroom. Each year I start my U.S. history survey course with a brief unit on "Monuments, Memorials, and Commemoration." I use this unit to start the year, because I will use public monuments and memorials the entire year as we work our way through the American saga. In order to do this, it is essential to provide students with sufficient background information so that the study of monuments occurs within a context. Monuments and sculpture help me augment my classes and the essential themes and objectives that I teach about U.S. history. They serve not only as tangible reminders of the past, but also in the case of those monuments and memorials erected today, tell us something about our particular time and place in history. For instance, recently the design of the *Franklin D. Roosevelt Memorial* was embroiled in controversy: Should the statue portray

Roosevelt in a wheelchair or not? I videotaped a *Dateline* broadcast about the issue to show my class. When the broadcast was over, we had a lively discussion about the controversy. Some students viewed the inclusion of the wheelchair as a case of extreme political correctness. Others felt that the wheelchair was appropriate because Roosevelt was, in fact, confined to one. As we talked, students began to see that there is no "right" answer to the problem—and that this tension is inherent in democracy itself.

You can conduct a similar exercise, encouraging students to voice their own opinions using either a past or current controversy over a monument (national or local). Ask students why they think the monument is being created in the first place, and what they think it says about society (or the people who support the monument). If you are dealing with a monument that is already in place, ask them if they think its design might be different today, and if so why. Discuss aspects of symbolism in the monument, and how they reflect the culture.

Using public sculpture as a teaching tool makes sense. It's the most pluralistic art form we have. One can find men, women, blacks, whites, Hispanics, Asians, and American Indians gracing our public spaces all over the country. I not only refer to the better known pieces like French's *Abraham Lincoln* and the *Statue of Liberty*, but also to the countless monuments and memorials from Vermont to New Mexico. My use of sculpture in my classes has indeed made the works of art allies and friends in communicating the values, ideals, and history of our nation.

If you don't have access to a monument or site that you want to discuss—or you can't take your class there—don't despair. Many sites offer slides or photographs, or you can visit the site yourself and take pictures. The Saint-Gaudens site helped by sending me slides and photos. Once I received the slides and photographs from Saint-Gaudens National Historic Site, I worked them into my lessons. I told the students that we would take a look at something new, something different. I was hoping that the maxim about students getting excited by their teachers enthusiasm would hold true as I prepared to discuss Saint-Gaudens and his sculpture. It did! They responded well to the visual images of two works in particular, the *Shaw Memorial* and the *Adams Memorial*. They liked the *Shaw* because of its liveliness and the *Adams Memorial* because of its mysterious aura. I watched the faces of the students intently as I conducted the lesson. As they viewed the pictures, I asked them, "What do you think the significance of this angelic figure is?" and "Why do you think that the head is hooded in the *Adams Memorial*?"

The process of getting students to "buy into" something different requires a bit of salesmanship. I teach most of my material this way. I want my students to witness my desire to continue the learning process. I remember how impressionable I was at their age. I remember what and

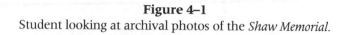

Figure 4–1
Student looking at archival photos of the *Shaw Memorial*.

who inspired me. Teenagers want to learn new things, they want to be taught in creative ways.

Reading and Writing About Sculpture

Another way to help students get the most out of their experience with sculpture is to expose them to materials written about it. Since I was personally interested in the work of Saint-Gaudens, I pursued everything about him and his work I could get my hand on. I invited Burke Wilkinson, a noted author on Saint-Gaudens, to speak to my students. Wilkinson accepted. Before his visit, I showed videos about Saint-Gaudens and expanded on our previous discussions. When Wilkinson arrived, he

shared with students his methods for digging up biographical information—and he read passages from his own book. The students were
enthralled, both by Saint-Gaudens and by Wilkinson—a double success!

Talking about sculpture is good; writing about it takes the learning
process one step farther. Students may groan at the suggestion, but writing will help them make their own discoveries about sculpture and history. I had my students write about a particular Saint-Gaudens work, the
Adams Memorial. The memorial is located in Washington, D.C., and is one
of the best-known private memorials in the nation. (It was commissioned
by historian and journalist Henry Adams, after his wife's death by suicide.
After it was installed in 1890, Adams remarked "Saint-Gaudens has held
up the mirror and no more.") The memorial is timeless, like so much of
Saint-Gaudens' work. On viewing the sculpture, it's difficult to tell
whether the figure is a man or a woman; Saint-Gaudens modeled the
image from both male and female models. The mysterious image is
draped in a hooded cloak, whose folds mask the identity of the figure.
The right hand is gracefully positioned against the figure's chin, and the
eyes are closed.

One student wrote about the *Adams Memorial*

The *Adams Memorial* stands in its grove of trees and bushes, acting like
a door to the inside of the viewer's mind. The instant he sees the
monument, his imagination is catapulted in any of a thousand directions. His emotions swell like the rising cap of a shore bound wave.
He is drawn in closer, his eyes reach out to touch it, his soul runs
around the delicate curves, the contour of the lips, the rolling shape
of the cloak. He gazes in awe at the massive size of the object, physically and spiritually. Its statement, though totally unique to each
individual, is strong, thick and whips through him like a biting wind.
He suddenly becomes uncomfortable with this boundless freedom.
He feels a fluttering in his stomach, and gropes for something to hold
on to. Something to direct his shooting imagination, a title, a name,
an inscription of any kind. Nothing. He comes to a fork in the road.
Does he stop, closing his mind for fear of following a completely
wrong train of thought? Or does he shove the fear aside, taking a
running leap skyward, letting the bronze mirror's question, answer,
meaning and pith swirl about him as he soars further from the physical statue into the emotional universes which it reflects back at him.
He comes across an obstacle which will always block him. He feels
the desperate urge to share what he feels with someone. To include
another in his imaginary journey. He reaches deep inside himself for
exactly the right word, or phrase, but can find none. He tries anyway,
forming a sentence in his mind, but realizes that even the best, most
eloquent account only serves to tie his feeling down. He feels an
inkling of loneliness, realizing that there are simply no words known
to man in any tongue which describe the emotional mushroom he is
experiencing. That is when his question becomes an answer. That is

why it was sculpted out of bronze because there are no words. The price of its beauty is whatever he discovers, he must discover alone.

Another student wrote,

> Saint-Gaudens had no definite theme in mind when he sculpted the *Adams Memorial*. Rather his statue inspires a range of emotions in the viewer. The statue is hauntingly appealing. Its compelling form makes a strong impression. The beauty of Saint-Gaudens' work is that his statue inspires so many different ideas, thoughts, questions, and possible titles. The title *Mystic Contemplation* could easily fit this statue. The position of the hands gives the impression of a pondering or thoughtful pose. And there is a certain mysterious aura. *The Peace That Passeth Understanding* and *The Mystery of the Hereafter* could also apply. The popular theme of an overlapping spiritual and physical world is demonstrated in these two titles for the statue. The person in the statue is wrapped in a shroud which conjures up a picture of a religious being. Saint-Gaudens' statue successfully evokes a variety of feelings rather than one specific emotional response. If living today, Saint-Gaudens would probably smile with delight at the veritable wealth of feelings his statue elicits.

Students learn by examining the *Adams Memorial* how the concept of death was interpreted by some during the Victorian Era. Yet they also have to face the reality that the statue still means the same thing today, more than one hundred years after it was unveiled in 1890. I want them to think about time and space—why has the meaning of this work not really changed much in a century? How close are we in time to the late nineteenth century? What events since then might have changed our nation, but not necessarily the value and timeless quality of this particular work? Students also learn by writing about this subject how art shapes human perception—in this case, the theme of death.

Whenever we visit the memorial, I always relate its story to set it in proper context. The sculpture does a wonderful job of prompting students to think critically. And again, since the piece is open to such a wide latitude of interpretation I like to ask students to "name" the work. The answers often vary and reflect, as well they should, the students' experiences. It is as if their thoughts are living proof of Henry Adams' reflection mentioned above. Those students who have gone out on their own usually report back to me with statements like, "It was really cool."

My interest in the connection between one sculpture and history led me to other sculptors and their works. I began to branch out with my enthusiasm locating or discovering other pieces of public sculpture that would work in the classroom. Over the years, I have amassed an extensive slide collection that reflects not only my personal interest in particular works, but also works that are helpful in teaching U.S. history. As such I have been able to build a curriculum around a specified framework outlining the American drama. I began to deliberately look in the *Washington Post* for articles that I could use in my classroom work. Currently this nation is experiencing a boom in monumental commemoration. Not since the years after the Civil War has this country seen such an explosion of commemorative monuments. In part, this is due to the national need to honor those who fought in Vietnam, and a desire in the Black community to honor their lost heroes, such as the Buffalo Soldiers, who were featured in a monument raised at Fort Leavenworth, Kansas in 1992. Assorted civil rights memorials have cropped up in the south. A monument has been proposed for The Mall honoring Black Patriots of the American Revolution, and the *National Memorial to Black Soldiers and Sailors of the Civil War* was unveiled in the summer of 1998 in the Shaw neighborhood of Washington, D.C. In addition, the establishment of the Save Outdoor Sculpture Project, sponsored by the Smithsonian, whose aim is to identify those outdoor sculptures that are in need of restoration and conservation and compile a database list of all pieces of outdoor sculpture in the United States has also raised national consciousness. Plenty of newspaper and magazine articles report these stories that I find useful in the classroom in getting students to see and understand the relevance of commemorative monuments.

During the 1980s, seemingly endless debate raged in the press over the *Vietnam Memorial*. During this time period there were all sorts of musings in the papers about the need for a separate sculpture recognizing women who served in Vietnam. One letter to the editor argued, with great sincerity, that a statue to the K-9 Corps should be added because many dogs lost their lives in Vietnam. This letter really got my classes going. Most students groaned that all of this "stuff" was getting way out of hand. I was able to use this as a teachable moment to explore the concept of democracy and the inherent tension that exists when people have divergent views on an issue. Some students felt that the *Wall* should have been left alone and that adding the figurative sculptures only opened a Pandora's Box. However, most of the girls in my classes felt that since the statue of the *Three Servicemen* had been added then it was only fair that women should have their own piece. In one very heated debate one student said, "Look, the *Wall* includes the names of over 58,000 people of which only eight are women. It should be left as that. Eight women do not need their own statue." The girls in the class objected loudly. I had to remind everyone that the *Vietnam Veterans Memorial* was meant as not only a tribute to those who died in Vietnam, but also to those who served and returned home. In this exchange between students the debate that raged at the national level was being acted out in my classroom. It was a great day to be a teacher.

Another avenue to take with this is the issue of the artist's rights. I ask students to think about how the designer of the *Wall*, Maya Lin, must have felt with the additions to her original design? Doesn't the artist have any say over changes? Is national consensus more important than the artist's original intent? What does this say about our society and our values? Because this was a national debate the story of the creation of the *Vietnam Veterans Memorial* was covered nationally in newspapers and periodicals. Books have been written about this memorial, complete with discussions regarding the numerous controversies. Plenty of research material is available for any teacher to create comparable lessons. Check for back issues of *Time* and *Newsweek* in the *Guide to Periodicals*. Using public sculpture in this fashion can take you and your classes off in any number of directions.

"Clay Day"—A Chance for Students to Be Sculptors

Once students have viewed, discussed, and written about historical sculpture, you can enhance their learning experience by giving them a taste of what it's like to *be* a sculptor. You aren't teaching an art class; you are giving students a chance to try molding an idea or philosophy into something people can see and touch. At the end of the introductory unit on commemorative monuments, after we have looked at the history of monuments in general, and their purpose and symbolism, I provide each student with a pound of clay. (I order the clay during the previous spring. If you purchase it in bulk the cost is much lower.) I tell the students to model or mold any image they want. It may be real or abstract in design. It's a great exercise because the students begin to understand that art is something that doesn't just happen. Like anything of value or merit it takes hard work and planning. I want my students to recognize that the sculptor must first start with an idea and somehow take this idea and transfer it into reality. I stand back and watch them take this pound of clay and work hard at getting it malleable in their hands. I watch them struggle with the initial question they almost all have of, "What should I make?" It takes some time for them to get going. The clay is not easy to work with. It's hard and inflexible until their body temperature warms it up to where it can be shaped. Many students are afraid that I will evaluate them on their artistic merits. Nothing could be further from the case. Since writing and keeping journals is part of my method of student assessment, their assessment for this activity will be based on the writing in their journals—not their creations. Some students are very good at it and have created whimsical figures, surfboarders, or basketball players while others have created musicians playing the guitar or drums. I'm not really looking for anything specific. I want them to work through the process of coming up with an idea and seeing that idea become a reality.

Figure 4–2
A student creates something on Clay Day.

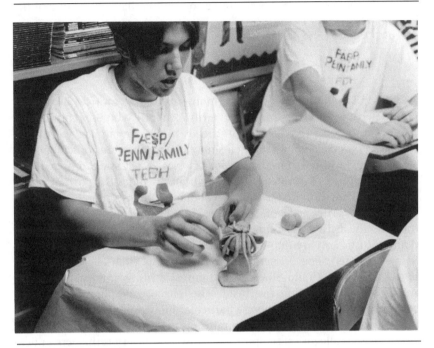

When they write their journal responses, the students almost universally record that they have a new appreciation for the artist and his or her craft. What once looked easy is now appreciated as hard, thoughtful work. In many ways this activity helps them to appreciate the sculpture I show during the rest of the year. They understand it better and can more easily appreciate the work and the process. When I survey my classes in June with my year-end evaluation, many students tell me that "Clay Day" was the best day of the year and the one that they will most remember.

As a follow-up to this, many students naturally then ask "How do the large pieces get created?" For this answer I turn to two films. The Saint-Gaudens National Memorial Trust produced a film, *Wax Blood. Bronze Skin* that shows how the *Farragut* Memorial was recast using the lost-wax process—a highly complex skill. This film demonstrates the step-by-step process in casting bronze sculpture. The second film is the Academy Award–winning documentary, *The Stonecarvers*, that describes using the words of the craftsmen the process of bringing clay models into full size marble figures. Both films work well with students, and I deliberately use them to point out the highly interdisciplinary nature of creating monumental public sculptures. Students come to understand the importance of knowing mathematics and science to create something that reflects one of the humanities.

Using Commemorative Works

As you and your students study monuments and memorials, it's important to become familiar with certain terms. Anyone who uses commemorative monuments to teach history needs to also be familiar with these terms. *Portrait sculpture* is simply a singular portrait of an individual. *The Seated Lincoln* by French in the *Lincoln Memorial* is a classic example of this type of sculpture. *Portrait-allegorical* sculpture includes the portrait of the individual being honored along with additional figures representing concepts or ideas. These allegorical figures are called *ideal figures* because they interpret the artist's embodiment of that particular ideal, be it virtue, freedom, or justice. Many times allegorical figures are represented by angels. Saint-Gaudens' *Shaw Memorial* is the ultimate portrait-allegorical work, depicting Robert Gould Shaw, ideal figures of his infantrymen, and the Angel of Death passing overhead. The purpose of portrait-allegorical sculpture is to tell a story about a particular individual. *Allegorical sculpture* relies strictly on ideal figures to communicate a story or value. *The Statue of Liberty* is an allegorical sculpture, because its imagery is the personification of the artist's, Auguste Bartholdi, interpretation of liberty.

I like to use all types of sculpture with my students, but allegorical sculptures are the best for getting students to think. One piece that I am very fond of is a memorial to Connecticut's Civil War prisoners of war, called *The Soldier Boy of Andersonville*, by sculptor Bella Pratt, a one-time student and assistant of Saint-Gaudens. I use this image after we have studied Civil War prisoner of war camps and exposed the students to the horrors of those camps. When I put the slide up on the screen, I ask students to try and identify what they think this figure is. It's a solitary young boy holding his hat in his left hand. His face conveys a message of sadness. He's lost and forlorn. This figure stands to represent all of those from the state of Connecticut who languished away in any number of Confederate POW compounds.

I ask the students to tell me what they see. What do they feel? What emotion does this piece draw out of them and why? I ask them if this sculpture does justice to the people who it honors. It is precisely these kinds of questions that are needed when you use any kind of monument or memorial in a classroom situation.

Another piece that works well with students is the *Shaw Memorial* by Saint-Gaudens. I like to use the *Shaw* because it has helped me build connections with my Black students. This is a very powerful work and its existence today speaks to Black Americans. Dedicated in 1897 to Colonel Robert Gould Shaw and his men of the 54th Massachusetts Volunteer Infantry, the first official Black regiment of the Union Army. The story of Shaw and his men was best told recently by the motion picture *Glory*. But until that 1989 production, most of the world knew of the exploits of Shaw and his men through the Saint-Gaudens piece that sits on the top of Boston's Beacon Hill. The fact that Saint-Gaudens modeled over forty different Black images and used sixteen of them in the finished piece is critical in appreciating the depth of the work. The sculptor did not want a generic figure to represent the Black infantrymen of the 54th Massachusetts. He wanted distinct personalities. For a monument to be unveiled in America in 1897 with this kind of sensitivity is unique. For the first time in American art history the image of the African American created by a white male sculptor is noble and dignified. You can see this when you examine the individual soldiers. Several years ago one of my African-American students commented that she really liked the *Shaw* because of the statement she felt the sculpture made. Other Black students have felt that the foot soldiers get lost behind the figure of Shaw; they would prefer it if Shaw were not so prominent in the sculpture. This makes for a lively exchange between students. I do inform my students that in 1982, when the *Shaw Memorial* was restored, the names of the Black soldiers who lost their lives in the attack on Fort Wagner were inscribed on the back alongside the names of the fallen White officers whose names had been inscribed one hundred years ago.

Finally, using the *Shaw Memorial* goes a long way to show the interdisciplinary nature of history. This sculpture has inspired poetry like Robert Lowell's "For the Union Dead." It has inspired music like Charles Ives' piece "The Saint-Gaudens in Boston Commons" in his *Three Places in New England*, and more recently it has been in motion pictures like *Glory*. Generally, I look at the *Shaw Memorial*, in detail, during our study of the Civil War. I have found that combining the visual examination of the piece with the Ives' music and the Robert Lowell's poem helps students see the interrelationship between history and the arts. In order to do this, students need to have enough background information to make assessments. After we watch *Glory* I tell the students the background history of the *Shaw*, using slides of the memorial and archival images taken in Saint-Gaudens' studio and at the 1897 dedication. As we look at the slides we identify the various parts, such as the angel, the figure of Shaw himself, and the troops.

I also show students a sketch Saint-Gaudens made in the early stages of the creative process. It's a far different vision than the completed work. The sketch shows a lone equestrian. The Shaw family objected to this design on the grounds that Shaw was not a general, but a colonel: The family wanted him depicted with his men. I ask students to tell me which design works better for them—the completed work or the sketch. The final design almost universally gets the nod because the students see the story of Shaw and the 54th Massachusetts as being inextricably linked—to have him standing alone would only tell part of the story. For them the monument needs to represent the Black troops.

Once this is done I tell the students that we are going to listen to some American classical music inspired by the Saint-Gaudens sculpture—Charles Ives' "The Saint-Gaudens on Boston Common." Again, background material about the music is necessary to give the students some sort of context for the piece. For this I had to do some of my own background work researching Ives and his composition. I even went so far as to find out who the leading Ives scholar was so that I could speak with him. I think it's important to share with my students how I learned about the material by reaching out to other scholars thus modeling my lifelong commitment to learning and ways of obtaining information other than from encyclopedias or secondary works.

The Ives' piece is based on not only the sculpture, but also on some Stephen Foster songs and two tunes from the Civil War "Marching Through Georgia" and "The Battle Cry of Freedom." So before we listen to Ives we listen to these two songs so that the students can pick up on their melodies. Then, while keeping a slide of the *Shaw Memorial* on the screen, I play the nine-minute Ives' piece. When the music is finished, we discuss the arrangement and how it might be reflective of the sculpture. I ask students if they heard the strains of the two Civil War songs and if they can figure out why the music gets repeatedly loudly and then softly, then loudly and softly again. This was Ives' attempt to mirror the high and low relief of the sculpture. After we listen to the music, I have one of the students in our school's creative writing class come in and recite Lowell's "For the Union Dead." Once all of the components are in place students write in their journals. Then we have a class discussion on the various interpretations of the story of Shaw and the 54th Massachusetts Infantry. In closing I have students read Frederick Douglass' "Men of Color, to Arms!" essay. Then I read excerpts from various speakers at the 1897 dedication, including the remarks of Booker T. Washington. For closure, students write a dedication of their own had they been invited to the 1897 Memorial Day ceremony. I use journal writing for assessment purposes; I look for what the students learned and if they internalized both the significance of the historical context of the sculpture and the detail.

It is my hope that after my students have studied with me, they will be able to see the world around them in a new way. I want to open their eyes so they can find for themselves a vision of their own life—to find what calls them in the same way I have found the spirit of Saint-Gaudens calling out to me to be who I am in the classroom.

Saint-Gaudens has been my own inspiration, but there are many other sculptors who have created equally compelling pieces about U.S. history that can be of value and use in the classroom. In addition to the Connecticut POW memorial, mentioned before, I have used public sculptures of American Indians and pioneer women to teach lessons. In both these cases, I have used slides or photos because I couldn't visit the monuments myself.

Much public sculpture of American Indians tends to be sympathetic to their story. The two principal sculptors of the image of the "noble" American Indian are James Earle Fraser, another assistant and student of Saint-Gaudens, and Cyrus Dallin. Both sculptors' masterpieces have to do with the "defeated" Indian. Fraser created *The End of the Trail* and Dallin sculpted *The Appeal to the Great Spirit*. The original intent for *The End of the Trail* was for it to be placed in San Francisco, on a cliff overlooking the Pacific Ocean. The dejected Indian and his exhausted mount having no place farther to go represent the complete defeat of all Indian nations. Their placement symbolizes the loss of a people and an entire continent. Had these plans worked as Fraser had hoped, the monument might have been even more powerful than it is. The final version ended up in a park in Waupun, Wisconsin, because a local patrician felt that it was an important work that needed a place; subsequently this individual purchased Fraser's work for his community. I was able to get background information from the Waupun Public Library and secured some slides from the Cowboy Hall of Fame in Oklahoma City.

The *Appeal* by Dallin sits in front of the Boston Museum of Fine Arts, which sells slides of the statue for a nominal fee. In this monumental work, an Indian Chief sits astride his horse, head raised upward and back, arms outstretched, beseeching the Great Spirit to answer his prayers or supplications.

I like to use these images with my classes after we have studied the American Indian situation in detail, including an examination of the Creek Wars (1814) and the Battle of Horseshoe Bend, the Cherokee Trail of Tears, the story of Chief Joseph and the Nez Perce as documented in the film *I Will Fight No More Forever* (1976), and the film *In the White Man's Image*, the story of the Carlisle Indian School from the American Experience series. Following all of this material, students study the slide images and then examine a political cartoon relating to the Indian question. I ask them to think about these two sculpted interpretations in light of what they have learned. Again they reflect their thoughts in journal writing. Most students are able to see clearly the meaning of these two works. Comments both in their journals and in follow-up discussion almost invariably include phrases like: "These sculptures really show what the Indians went through." "*The End of the Trail* looks like the Indian is worn out, totally dejected and defeated—it's sad." Some students agree that *The*

End of the Trail would in fact work better in San Francisco. As for the *Appeal* students are drawn to the helpless look on the chief's face. Many students feel that this sculpture has a hint of hope in it for the Indian, because as they see it this Indian at least has one more avenue to pursue in asking the Great Spirit for help.

These two images draw a sensitivity out of my students that might not have been possible had they not been exposed to these powerful figures. I also show a slide of a work produced by Horatio Greenough in 1832 called *The Rescue*. This work formerly stood at the top of the main entrance staircase on the East Front of the U.S. Capitol. When restoration of the East Front took place in the 1960s this sculpture was removed, partially at the request of American Indian organizations. I ask students to compare this image—which is blatantly stereotypical, showing a frontiersman subduing a "savage Indian" from attacking his family—with the interpretations of Indians as depicted by Fraser and Dallin. I ask them why they think the works by Fraser and Dallin are more sympathetic. Why would the artists separated by less than one hundred years have distinctly different views of a group of people and their story? What might the artists' motivation be? Students pick up on the fact that at the time the Greenough was placed in the Capitol, the United States was beginning to really push west. It was easier to take the land if those you were taking it from were demonized. Teachers who choose this or a similar activity can also launch into a discussion with students as to how the location of a monument can affect its meaning.

Several years ago I was given a slide of a sculpture in Ponca City, Oklahoma, called *The Pioneer Woman* (1930) by Bryant Baker. I discovered that the sculpture was part of a museum complex called The Pioneer Woman Museum. I called the museum and asked if they could send me some additional material for classroom use. They sent me newspaper clippings about the dedication, a copy of Will Rogers' dedication speech, and a small booklet containing images of all the sculptures that were entered in the competition for *The Pioneer Woman* statue. They also included a copy of the speech given by Oklahoma Governor E. W. Marland at the dinner he hosted for the competing sculptors.

I created a lesson plan on the movement west based on the material they sent me and the Ric Burns film, *The Donner Party*. I provided the students with background into the life experiences of pioneer women and read them the speech given by Governor Marland. Next, I passed out pictures of the eleven pieces entered in the competition and asked students to do two things: 1) select the image from the models that best represented their interpretation of the pioneer woman and 2) determine which one was the eventual winner. The students both discussed and debated the questions; when I finally revealed the competition winner, those who had chosen it gloated. This lesson proves the power of interpretation when it comes to history as the same concept, or in this case image, can mean different things to different people. It also provides an opportunity to explore the role of women in frontier society and any stereotypes that might be portrayed in the sculpture entries. I ended this particular lesson by showing slides of yet another statue of a pioneer woman—the *Memorial to the Pioneer Mother,* in Kansas City. I asked students to tell me which statue now best defined their idea of a pioneer woman. It was gratifying to see the changes in their perceptions between the first discussion and this final one.

You can do this same exercise with any group of statues you choose, using the discussion to probe an issue or event in American history. Some possibilities include the Revolutionary War, using Daniel Chester French's *Minute Man* (1875); racial discrimination, as memorialized by Maya Lin's *Civil Rights Memorial* (1989); exploration and settlement of the West, depicted in a host of sculptures commemorating the Lewis and Clark Expedition; or immigration, memorialized by Luis Sanguino's *The Immigrants* (1973).

I have found that using sculpture in the study of Abraham Lincoln is especially productive. This requires providing students with a great deal of background material; it should be taught after the political and military dimensions of the war have been covered. Students need also to be exposed to Lincoln's most crucial speeches, *The House Divided Speech,* some excerpts from his debates with Stephen Douglas, *The Gettysburg Address,* and both *Inaugural Addresses.* Most standard U.S. history textbooks include these particular speeches. My students listen to various recordings of Lincoln's speeches and then we discuss the important content of each oration. In a short lecture, I tell students about Lincoln's life. I talk about Lincoln the man, his life, and the struggles he endured as a human. I tell my students that had Lincoln been alive today he would be diagnosed as suffering from depression, that he had a high-pitched, squeaky voice with a frontier twang, and that his marriage to Mary Todd Lincoln was often strained.

I admit that I'm a Lincolnophile. I have spent several years photographing sculpted images of Lincoln and have a number of interpretations in my collection. For this activity I use ten images covering the range of Lincoln, the man and the myth, from his youth through his presidency. For reference and background I draw material out of Merill D. Peterson's book, *Lincoln in American Memory,* Stephen B. Oates' biography, *With Malice Toward None,* Benjamin P. Thomas' *Abraham Lincoln,* and David Herbert Donald's *Lincoln.*

Abraham Lincoln has been depicted in sculpture more than any other American. The sculptures, found throughout the country, show many different interpretations of the man. My images include French's *Lincoln* in the *Lincoln Memorial,* Saint-Gaudens *Standing Lincoln* in Chicago,

George Gray Barnard's *Lincoln the Candidate* in Cincinnati, Anna Hyatt Huntington's *Lincoln on the Prairie* in New Salem, Illinois, and Gutzon Borglum's *Seated Lincoln* in Newark, New Jersey, among others. To obtain your images consider tapping into the Inventory of American Sculpture at the National Museum of American Art, available on the Internet.

First I put the images of Lincoln up on the screen. I tell students that in 1860 the artist, Leonard Volk, made a life mask of Lincoln and created casts of his hands and that all sculptors who have sculpted Lincoln have used these casts (which were replicated) to create their impressions of the sixteenth President. When we're finished looking at the images, I play composer Aaron Copland's *Lincoln Portrait*. Recordings of this can be found in many good libraries and music stores. I use the version with the Gregory Peck narration, which is fifteen minutes. When it is finished we again take up the discussion of interpretation of the subject, including why Americans seem to require a person with a deep, eastern-sounding voice to read Lincoln's words. Students really get into it and again they have differing viewpoints. Some prefer Lincoln the railsplitter, while others like Lincoln the country lawyer. Whatever their reactions and impressions, they construct for themselves their own history based on a total integration of the senses. These are some of the insights students have imparted to me: "I like the work by French in the *Lincoln Memorial* because it is so huge that it reflects his power as President." Another student said, "The one of Lincoln as the railsplitter is good because it shows Lincoln picking up his law book and leaving behind his ax to move on with his life. Had he not done this he wouldn't have become president." Still another student surmised, "The Saint-Gaudens in Chicago works best for me because it is highly detailed and shows Lincoln thinking about something before he is going to speak. Since his speeches were important it makes sense to have a sculpture like this."

Create Your Own Portfolio

I'm so excited about using sculpture as a teaching tool that I think I have images of just about every major theme in U.S. history and try to incorporate them into the overall context of American history where they fit. To start your own portfolio, contact the National Museum of American Art and ask them for their kit called "Public Sculpture: America's Legacy." It contains slides, a videotape, and a lesson plan book with specific lessons. If you have access to the Internet, try a little surfing on the World Wide Web for images that may be available. Another good source of images is the Index of American Sculpture housed at the University of

Delaware. If you live in or near a major metropolitan area, contact the local municipal art society. Most major cities have published guides to their public art and sculpture that are also quite helpful. Some suppliers offer digital images at low costs to educators.

In addition I assisted the education department of the National Gallery of Art with their website for the Gallery's installation of the 1901 cast of the *Shaw Memorial* (this was Saint-Gaudens' fourth and final version.) This site has additional material related to the *Shaw Memorial* including other lesson plans that you can use. Saint-Gaudens National Historic Site also has a home page with an educational link. I have also published through the National Park Service a "Teaching with Historic Places" lesson plan on Saint-Gaudens National Historic Site.

Another source for you to consider is Brookgreen Gardens, in Murrell's Inlet, South Carolina. This is the location of the largest outdoor sculpture garden in the United States. Prominent works by many of the sculptors mentioned in this chapter are on display there. The staff of Brookgreen Gardens has published a wonderful workbook, complete with reproducible worksheets on how to use sculpture in the classroom. They also sell strip slides that, in many cases, duplicate the pieces found in the workbook. Educational resource sheets can also be sent to you that include a glossary of sculpture terms and other useful information.

Another technique that I have used is to take slides of sculptures from books. Using my standard 35 mm camera with a macro lens, I either attach it to a photographic copy stand or go out on my deck, being sure to hold the camera very still—you might want to use a tripod—and shoot slide images from large, colorful sculpture catalogues. Most major American sculptors have had coffee-table books published about them and their work. If your library does not have them you can always secure these books through Interlibrary loan.

Take your camera and wander around your own community. Are there any monuments and memorials that you can take your students to study and see? Local historical societies or library reference rooms often have the primary source documents available for you to put together the history of these works.

One of the best discoveries I made while looking for information on statues was the AAA Road Guides. In the back of each book there is an index that lists the topic "Statues." Telephone the administrative office that manages the sculpture. Typically, monuments are maintained by the local park authority. This is how I was able to obtain slides of a Gutzon Borglum sculpture of William Jennings Bryan located in Salem, Illinois, and an image of Sakajawea by Alice Cooper in Portland, Oregon—among others. The city managers or park authority personnel I have talked with have been more than happy to fulfill my request, so the images are either free or come with a nominal charge.

Extended Learning Activities

The ways I've been able to incorporate sculpture into my classroom could be repeated anywhere in the United States with a little bit of flexibility and imagination. If you live in a major metropolitan area check those sources listed in the Appendix to help you see how you can shape your activity. If you do not live in an area that has much public sculpture, but have access to the Internet or World Wide Web then you, too, can fashion an activity along similar lines.

Some memorials have their own website. The planned memorial for the Oklahoma City Federal Building Bombing is now up on the web. Students can take a virtual tour of the proposed memorial to get a better sense of the design and the artist's intent. Since this is a contemporary memorial tied to a contemporary issue, you can use it as a vehicle to launch into a discussion about public memory and recent history.

Since Washington, D.C., is rich in this kind of resource I like to send students out into the city's environs. Their mission: Locate and find a particular commemorative statue that has been assigned to them, visit it, photograph it, and then write about the subject and the piece. I have students pick a name of a sculpture out of a hat based on my knowledge of what statues are downtown and where they are located. These sculptures are all portrait sculptures of various people who have helped shape the history of the United States. The students are then required to do some mini-research on the person who has been represented in sculpture— they have to compile a list of biographical milestones: What did this person do? Why did they merit a sculpture, and what contributions did this person make to the history of the United States? After they take the photographs and write out important biographical data, they have to write in their journals about their experience. For many students it's really the first time they have explored Washington, D.C. They enjoy the experience. "Clay Day" now makes sense. They learn that not all learning takes place in a classroom, and their particular sculpture becomes *their* sculpture. They assume ownership of the piece and thereby own their own learning process. I request that they take two photographs of their assigned sculpture with them posing in the picture; one goes in their journal stapled alongside their written response and the other goes up on the wall in my classroom in Clio's Corner.

On the due date I enjoy watching the students come in with their photographs. Before I collect them, the room is abuzz with chatter as students share and exchange their pictures with one another. I ask them to talk about their visit and we hear all kinds of stories about how they drove "all over D.C. looking for their sculpture." In more ways than one it is a learning adventure. Many students tell me that for the first time in their life they actually came to appreciate sculpture and that until this assignment they hadn't even noticed that sculpture was part of their environment. I often hear from students that they now stop and look at monuments and no longer take them for granted—they know that these faded relics of our past national experience mean something to them and for time immemorial.

Students also learn about interpersonal relations from this activity. Some students work in groups going to visit more than one monument, so that they can share a roll of film and be with friends. This helps foster the sense of community in the classroom that I see as an important ingredient to my success as a teacher. Other students go with their parents. For them it turns out to be a family activity and directly involves the parent in their son's or daughter's learning experience. Some students have told me that they actually had a "good time" doing this assignment with one of their parents. This is also a way to build bridges to parents whom I view as important allies in the school environment.

As one last task, I ask students to count how many sculptures are of men and how many are of women. Currently only two portrait sculptures are found in Washington, D.C. to specific American women: One is of Mary McLeod Bethune and the other one is of Eleanor Roosevelt, as part of the *Franklin Delano Roosevelt Memorial*. The other sculptures dealing with issues in women's history are all allegorical figures representing a person or idea such as the three women figures added to the *Vietnam Veterans Memorial*. I ask students to tally up the number of images of men versus women and see who comes out ahead. Naturally they find an overwhelming number of male sculptures compared to female sculptures. As a class we talk about this and explore why it is so. It sets up my lesson down the road on the *National Women's Rights Memorial* and the subsequent controversial issues that are tied with this sculpture.

Now, how can you accomplish this in your classroom? Those of you living near major metropolitan areas will have it easy. For those of you not so fortunate here's the game plan. Choose an event in American history, let's say the Revolutionary War or the Civil War—I'm using these because I know that an abundant amount of sculpture across the country is dedicated to these two time periods. Using either the Internet, the Web, or one of the other sources I have discussed, compile a list of different individuals who are represented in sculpture. Have students draw names out of a hat in the same fashion as I do and then ask them to conduct similar kinds of research. The questions I framed above can be used. Instead of sending them into Washington, D.C., send them out into the world of the World Wide Web to pull together their research. After they have completed their research and have obtained an image of their particular sculpture, have them report back to the class about their work of art and its sculptor. Using newsprint that can be displayed around the classroom, have the students list their commemorated individual, along with the contributions that person made to the history of the United States. Be certain that the students explain why this person earned a statue and attach an image of their sculpture. Once students report to the class have the class as a whole walk around and look at this "Hall of Fame" that they have created. If you have twenty-five students in your class, you will, in using this activity, have covered twenty-five noteworthy Americans.

If you use this activity with your study of the Civil War, you will no doubt come across heroes and heroines of the Confederacy. Here you can seize the "teachable moment" and discuss with your students the appropriateness and merit of having statues in the United States that commemorate and honor the defenders of slavery.

For a final year-end project, students can pick one person from American history and design a monument or memorial to that person. I require that they base their design on the types of sculpture that we had discussed earlier in the year—namely portrait, allegorical, or portrait-allegorical. The personalities students have selected to memorialize range from Amelia Earhart to Walt Disney. In addition they have to come up with some ideas as to what kind of memorial they would like to see created to themselves. This gives them a chance to explore all kinds of possibilities and give some thought to their futures.

If you are willing to put the time in by doing the necessary background reading and research on these topics—from the fundamental understanding of sculpture to the memorial-specific topic—then the use of sculpture with your students will convey American history like no other technique. As a song once suggested, it's true a "bronze man can still tell stories." At least that's what I like to think as I sit on the steps of Saint-Gaudens' final resting place watching the sun dip below the trees.

Five

Guest Speakers and Telephone Conferences

"What is the use of a book," thought Alice, *"without pictures or conversations?"*

Lewis Carroll
Alice's Adventures in Wonderland

Their names are Warrant Officer Bill Troy, Private First Class Bill Rolen, and Sergeant Wayne Hitchcock. If you were to meet them on the street, you would think that they were ordinary men, enjoying their golden years. Yet these men were part of history, and the twentieth century's greatest drama, World War II, because they are part of a small minority of soldiers who spent time during the war in either German or Japanese prisoner of war camps. Fortunately for me and my students, they have been willing to share their experiences with my classes and, in doing so, allowed us to encounter history in a fashion that no textbook could provide.

This chapter is concerned with creating a classroom environment that in part relies on guest speakers meeting with students and helping them see that history does not occur in a vacuum; rather, history is the lives of real people. This chapter will also provide ideas for you to use in setting up telephone conferences between you, your students, and someone who can't personally visit your classroom, but who is willing to spend time talking over a speakerphone discussing their experiences and expertise. In either case, you and your students can enjoy a rich experience.

Guest Speakers

Planning is essential. Think through your objectives and what you want your students to learn. Be sure to prepare your students in advance about who they will be speaking with and what topic the speaker is going to present to them. Try to schedule speakers so that when they visit your classroom their topic is of relevance to the curriculum you are currently studying. In addition, consider your choice of evaluative and assessment techniques to ensure that your students synthesize the material that was presented to them. I like to have students complete a journal entry in which I read all of their reactions. We also follow up any activity like this with a debriefing and discussion session.

In the case of the three former POWs from World War II, my own interest in their experience came from my research into this aspect of American history. This, in turn, stemmed from my experiences working with the National Park staff at Andersonville National Historic Site. The prison camp and National Cemetery at Andersonville, Georgia, is also the home of the *American National Prisoner of War Memorial* and Museum. Andersonville National Historic Site's mission is not only to interpret the role of the Civil War prison that was located there from 1864 to 1865, but also to interpret the story of all of America's prisoners of war from the War for Independence to the Persian Gulf War. I had been introduced to some former prisoners of war on one of my visits to the site and decided to call the American Ex–Prisoner of War organization in Washington, D.C., to see if any of these veterans, living in my area, would be willing to speak with my classes.

Preparation

To prepare students for the visit by the three former POWs, I asked them to imagine what it might be like to be a prisoner of war. How might they feel? What circumstances might they encounter? How did they think that they might react to being denied absolute freedom? These questions were a foreshadowing of issues that the ex-prisoners of war would touch upon. The students are also provided with a handout of quotes about or by prisoners of war. Most of the quotes are from *Voices from Captivity* by Robert C. Doyle. All of this is done to prepare students better for the meeting and to get them to listen with some empathy.

Without giving too much detail, I told the students that these men were captured by either the Germans or the Japanese and spent considerable time behind barbed-wire fences. We also discussed the American Ex-Prisoner of War Association to which these men belong. Finally, I provided students with some statistics about this organization and World War II. Currently, more than 55,000 ex-American prisoners of war are still alive. Most of these men and women are World War II veterans, along with veterans from the Korean and Vietnam Wars. A tightly knit community of survivors, they have endured more than most humans would think possible. They want their story told, as it sometimes gets lost among the hundreds of historical narratives about battles, campaigns, and generals. It is important that the students know this information beforehand so that they can keep the experiences of these individuals in context to both the past as well as the present. It is also important to remind students to be respectful when the speakers are in the classroom and to remember that these individuals are giving of their own time. It has been my experience that in cases where you have speakers visit, students are usually on their best behavior.

The Classroom Visit

On the day that the three ex–prisoners of war visited my classes, I made sure that they arrived with plenty of time to spare before class started. This allowed us to get a little better acquainted and gave them a chance to get comfortable. Before the class started, I wrote each of the individual's names on the board so that students could refer to them by name when necessary.

Since my school teaches in the block format, students can spend an extended period of time with speakers. After I introduced the visitors to my class, I explained how we would proceed. Each individual would speak for fifteen to twenty minutes, presenting his particular story. After the men told their stories, I opened the floor for questions, which left approximately forty minutes for student questions.

All three men came attired in their organization's maroon blazers and sporting their service caps. Bill Troy, because he is confined to a wheelchair, was accompanied by his wife, whose name I also wrote on the board.

Bill Rolen, who is President of the American Ex–Prisoners of War organization, was seventeen years old when he joined the service in 1943. His infantry unit participated in the American landings at Anzio Beach, fought up the Italian boot, and was present at the American liberation of Rome in 1944. Bill also was part of Operation Anvil, which was the Allied invasion of southern France (an often forgotten campaign of the war). It was shortly after this that his outfit was captured in eastern France near the Swiss border in August 1944. He spent seven months in a German POW compound.

Wayne Hitchcock was also a young man when his B-17 was shot down over France in 1944. He was a tail gunner who was lucky enough to survive his plane's crash. He spent thirteen months in a German camp.

Bill Troy was in his thirties when he served on General Douglas Mac-Arthur's staff in the Philippines. After MacArthur fled to Australia in the spring of 1942, Troy remained behind on the island of Corregidor serving with MacArthur's second in command General Jonathan Wainwright. He was present when Wainwright surrendered the last American outpost in the Philippines to the Japanese. Although he did not participate in the infamous Battan Death March, he did witness some of the horrible atrocities committed by Japanese soldiers on American and Philippine troops. He was shipped to Japan and spent three years laboring in a Japanese copper mine. For a period of time he was confined on an infamous Japanese "Hell Ship," which was a type of ship that held POWs. These ships were unmarked as carrying POWs and were used to lure American subs to unknowingly sink their own men. Fortunately for Bill he survived the ordeal and was liberated when the war came to its end in 1945.

My students were spellbound as the men related their stories. I sat where I could see both the faces of my students and the faces of the veterans.

Bill Rolen spoke first, giving the students some background information on the place of the American prisoner of war in history. He also spoke about his organization and their mission and goals, one of which is to maintain Andersonville National Historic Site as a perpetual shrine to the American prisoner of war. Rolen also gave students a glimpse of what it means to be involved in combat. He stated at the outset that nobody knows just how terrible combat is until they've experienced it. He agrees with William T. Sherman's maxim that "war is hell." His experience at Anzio alone proved that to him as he spoke with intentional restraint about the carnage of a battlefield. (Bill later confided to me that he did not want to get too graphic with his descriptions as it might upset the students.) Then Bill explained what happened to him and his unit as they were rounded up by German troops, loaded in boxcars, and shipped across Germany to an infantryman's Stalag. He explained to the students just how awful and frightening an experience this was. When he was captured, he weighed 137 pounds and when he was liberated he weighed 105—a result of the lack of food the Germans had by the end of the war. Bill also freely admitted that most prisoners of war had psychological issues to confront upon their return home.

Bill Troy opened his remarks with a reverie about the importance of living in a free society and that for some people the price of defending that freedom was a total loss of freedom. He told the students that there is no way to comprehend the reality of freedom until it is lost. With painstaking accuracy he told the details of the American surrender of Corregidor and how abusive the Japanese were to the defeated Americans. Most compelling of all was his story about how after Wainwright signed the instrument of surrender, that the General stood, with tears in his eyes,

Figure 5–1
POWs speaking. Bill Rolen *(l)* and Doug Idlett *(r)*.

turned and faced his men, and snapped a smart salute to his defeated comrades. In an expression of respect, Wainwright's men, including Troy, came to attention and saluted smartly back. The Japanese were amazed at this show of military protocol in the face of utter defeat. Fifty-five years after the event, Troy still was choked with emotion. He then related how as prisoners he and the other men were given little food, endured the transportation from the Philippines to the Japanese islands aboard a "Hell Ship," were forced to work hard labor in Japanese copper mines, and experienced horrendous living conditions. As a result of his imprisonment, he would be plagued with emphysema for the remainder of his life.

Wayne Hitchcock spoke to the students about what it's like to be shot out of the sky, and again related tales of being herded into boxcars, but it was his story of his comrades who did not survive the prisoner of war experience, and how he had to explain to one man's family why he survived and some did not that gripped the students. He could go no further as tears rolled down his cheeks. Many of the students, themselves, were on the verge of tears.

Once the veterans were finished, the students reacted with a flood of questions. The exchange between themselves and the generation that spoke to them was spellbinding. Most of the questions asked by the students were of a personal nature about what happened when they returned to the States, how their families reacted to their arrival, and what they did with their lives once the war was over. One student asked Troy directly about his views on the dropping of the atomic bombs. Without hesitation he responded that it was a blessing that had probably saved his life.

After a loud round of applause by my students, we all posed for pictures with the veterans. Naturally the photo would be placed in Clio's Corner. As a final token of their appreciation for having been invited to speak, the three veterans gave each student one 1995 U.S. commemorative stamp that was created to honor American prisoners of war. I was personally touched as the students eagerly waited to each receive their gifts. For me it was a moment when it seemed that both the veterans and the students had been gifts to each other.

Student Journals

Even though the experience in class was dramatic and moving, it was not until I read the students' journal entries on their reactions to the guest speakers that I comprehended how much they had internalized about their experience. All of the journal entries were sincere, well-thought out, and reflected a genuine concern for these men and what they had experienced. Some of the students had affixed the stamps they had received alongside their entry, adding another touching element to the experience. The journals themselves were a moving testimony not only to the ex-prisoners of war, but also to the students themselves as they grappled with just how horrible it can be learning about a historical reality from eyewitnesses.

One student wrote, "It was interesting that the men remembered everything they ate, including bugs, and that he could remember his hunger still today. Meeting people from the time brought all of the events from that time to life. They [the men's experiences] were descriptive and poignant. These men are heroes to me." Another student wrote,

> I would like to say how heroic these men were and still are. They were so articulate and poised and everything that made them speak so very special to me. I never knew my grandfathers, but one fought in the Pacific in World War II and was hit by a piece of shrapnel in the stomach. He healed himself of that, but I will never forget my

father telling the story that his father told him. Mr. Troy pointed out that you don't realize what a jewel freedom is and exactly means until you loose it. I can't imagine the mental anguish experienced in a camp like the ones those men were in. How horrible to never know if you will survive or die from the elements, or will get blown away out of humor by the Japanese. I am very glad that these veterans are speaking to people because the truth is that these people will all be gone—whereas our children will not be able to hear first hand accounts and emotional views of the war. One never gets that kind of information from a textbook or movie.

Still another student commented that she was appalled by the fact that in the case of Bill Rolen, he never changed his clothes once while a prisoner of war. Another student recorded, "I could listen to the Ex-POWS all day. The memories that they have are fascinating. I almost wish that I could have seen it for myself. Don't get me wrong, I don't want to go to war and be a POW. I just wish I could see some of the sights that they described. A fly-on-the-wall sort of thing." Finally, one student responded,

It makes a huge difference to hear an actual person tell you they were crammed into a boxcar with no food and water and no room to move rather than to merely read that it happened to someone. It made me think of my grandfather and other World War II vets I know who won't talk about what happened in Europe and Japan, and I wondered why the men we heard were able to while many cannot. While listening to their stories it suddenly occurred to me what Truman was faced with when deciding whether or not to drop the A-bomb. Thoughts of those very same men must have weighed heavily on his shoulders.

I have also had the former prisoners of war speak to my Applied History class. My intent here is to expose students to the actual prisoner-of-war experience before we take our field trip to Andersonville. While the format is the same as for my U.S. history class, I want the students to be able to make connections between the Civil War site and the reality of someone who did, in fact, experience life as a prisoner of war. On one occasion, a survivor of the Battan Death March, Doug Idlett, spoke to these students. As a twenty-three-year-old sergeant in the Army, he—as well as other American servicemen—were forced to walk 100 miles in nine days with little food and water. The students watched transfixed as he talked about the abuse he and his fellow soldiers experienced at the hands of their Japanese guards. Doug said that if you wanted to die all you had to do was lie down as either the climate conditions or the guards would ensure your death. For close to four years Doug worked at hard labor in a Japanese prison camp. When asked by one student about how he had survived such terrible conditions, he said that the main thing that kept him and those who survived with him alive was their faith in God. Putting it in a little bit of a different perspective Doug said, "Science says you can't live on what we were fed, yet we did, doing hard labor for almost four years." Powerful words to convey a powerful lesson.

If you are interested in having former American prisoners of war to speak with your classes, contact your local American Legion or Veterans of Foreign Wars post. Or contact the offices of the American Ex–Prisoners of War in Washington, D.C. They have a national list of all living American ex–prisoners of war and will be more than happy to assist you. Many World War II veterans are now willing to talk openly about their experiences. They know that they were a part of history and they want to tell their stories. For your classes they will provide what no book can, a human face of history.

Many people with special interests are more than willing to come and speak at schools or to specific classes. Many kinds of groups present living history, including period reenactors from Colonial America to the Civil War. Some of these interpreters have developed programs specifically to take into schools. If you contact your local historical society, community museum, or the local history collections or archives manager at your library, they will probably be able to point you in a direction that can help you secure guest speakers for your classes.

Telephone Conferences

Another successful technique that has worked with my students is an arranged telephone conference. I have used this method with my Applied History classes that have spoken at length with a number of individuals who are important in the history arena. While on the surface, it may appear that a phone conference is an impersonal strategy; if handled effectively, it can be just as rich and rewarding as having a guest speaker in your classroom. Since I began teaching Applied History, the class has held phone conferences with filmmaker Ken Burns, author and historian David McCullough, author and scholar Edward Linenthal, and a *very* long-distance phone conference with high school students at Padua College in Melbourne, Australia. Each experience added to the students' understanding of history and how people outside of their secondary education environment approach the practice of history.

Let me assert that in arranging these conferences it is imperative that you be flexible and work within the schedule of the person with whom you are going to speak. I believe that most people, even well-known and highly regarded individuals such as the ones with whom we have talked, are willing to assist teachers who are committed to their profession, passionate about history, and enthusiastic about their teaching. Students appreciate the fact that notables are willing to take time from their busy schedules to share their experiences with them. They recognize sincerity when they see and feel it.

Some people might think I'm crazy to approach celebrities to ask them for their assistance. But I learned early on in my teaching that most people want to have a positive impact on other individuals, particularly when it comes to working with a younger generation. If you are polite and diplomatic in your approach, you too can pull off wonderful and meaningful opportunities for your students.

Preparation is key to the success of a telephone conference. The first telephone conference that I arranged was with Ken Burns. I wrote to him at Florentine Films in Keene, New Hampshire. This was a year after his tremendous success with his epic public television series, *The Civil War*. I knew that in writing him and requesting to set up a conference I was taking a risk. By this time, Burns was a celebrity. I was familiar with his films prior to *The Civil War* and had used some of them in class, most notably *Brooklyn Bridge* and *The Statue of Liberty*. Using them had been quite successful with my students. I explained in my letter that the Applied History class was a new educational venture for me as well as for my students and I was wondering if he would be willing to take a part in our inaugural year, by speaking to my students as part of our unit on history through film. I told him what films the students would be watching and what related books they would be reading. I sent the letter in May of 1991 with the hopes of scheduling the conference for sometime late the following fall during the next school year. Within several weeks I received a letter from one of his assistants stating, "Ken would like to help out." I was ecstatic!

Preparation

To prepare for this experience we watched several episodes from *The Civil War, Brooklyn Bridge,* and *The Statue of Liberty*. The class also read some articles by Burns in which he explained how and why history and film can often have a symbiotic relationship. As a class we spent some time talking about the role of history films and how they shape human perception of past events and personalities. The students were directed to think about questions that they would like to ask Burns. In addition I told the students that the conference would last approximately forty-five minutes and that we would let Burns speak first, for approximately fifteen to twenty minutes, and then students would have an opportunity to ask questions.

The Conference with Ken Burns

The day finally arrived and we gathered in the principal's conference room around the speakerphone. I set myself up as moderator between Burns and the students, though I wanted them to ask the specific questions themselves. We started the conference with Burns providing an opening discussion about history and film and how he perceives his role in this arena. He told us that he viewed himself as primarily a filmmaker who works with historical subjects to tell about a particular subject. Burns also told us about other projects he was working on, including his film, *Baseball*. It was clear from his remarks that he saw all of the history of America as a continuum, so it was logical to do the film *Baseball* right after he finished *The Civil War*.

After his opening remarks Burns fielded questions. He enthusiastically replied to the various questions posed by myself as well as the students. One student asked, "How do you separate emotion from history?" To which Burns replied that this is perhaps one of the hardest aspects of getting wrapped up in the story of the past, because you naturally become close to some of the historical figures whom you are studying. Other questions dealt with how he selects stories that he would like to translate into film and whether or not he starts with a particular thesis and works on his film as one would write an expository paper. On all accounts he was respectful of the questions and the one hour time slot we had set aside moved very quickly.

One of the problems that I had with the students during this exchange was that some of the more timid students did not ask questions. It was the same few who kept raising questions. I decided then and there that I would take a different approach the next time I arranged a similar activity.

The Conference with Australian Students

The following year I had an opportunity, because of my good working relationship with the National Archives Education Branch, to have my Applied History students participate in a phone conference with students in Australia. This was part of the Fiftieth Anniversary Commemoration of World War II. I was to have my students conduct some research into the American participation in World War II in the South Pacific Theater, while the students in Australia researched the same topic. I assigned students to go out and interview World War II veterans, research the combat that took place, and investigate the World War II Australian–American Alliance. The actual conference was arranged by two Australians. History teacher Bob Lewis set up the link at our end, and in Australia the program was managed by Tim Gurry of Ryebuck Media.

Again, I made sure to cover the necessary background material to lead my students to a place where they could develop logical, historically based questions. I divided the class into teams that would research the various aspects of the topic. Some students conducted oral histories with World War II veterans, others combed the school and community libraries working on the campaigns of the South Pacific, while a third group explored the American home front during the war. Some of the students interviewed grandparents who were alive during the war in order to obtain information about the home front. Students also talked with historian Ed Bearss, who at that time was Chief Historian of the National Park Service. Bearss experienced extensive combat in the South Pacific and sustained a severe wound from Japanese machine-gun fire. This wound left him without the use of his right arm. He was more than happy to meet with the five students who were handling the combat aspect of the lesson. He gave those students a first-rate interview.

After two weeks of research, we gathered back in the principal's conference room at 7:30 P.M. It was 7:30 A.M. in Australia. In order to make the conference more personal, the students from Australia had mailed my students pictures of themselves. In turn, I faxed them photos of my students. So we sat around the table in Springfield, Virginia, with pictures of the Australian students around us. I was surprised at how excited and nervous my students were. In order to avoid the same issue that had come up with students who talked with Ken Burns, I made sure beforehand that each student had written out a particular question they wanted to ask. I allowed the three teams to select a spokesperson who would ask the bulk of questions per group, but encouraged all of the students to participate. At the appointed hour I placed the phone call, and for the next sixty minutes we talked. Fortunately for the school the phone bill was picked up by the Archives and Ryebuck Media.

If you are interested in creating a similar activity, try contacting one of the American embassies or the consulate of a foreign nation that was an Allied participant during World War II, such as Great Britain, France, or Australia for that matter. Perhaps you can work through these diplomatic channels to secure an interesting exchange between students. Check to see, if you are fortunate to make a connection, whether your school district will defray the cost. Oftentimes school systems put aside special moneys for just such purposes.

During this conference, students stuck to the assigned topics and issues for about forty-five minutes, comparing notes, items, and information they had learned during their research. What they learned is that both nations struggled with the war in much the same way. The students who researched the home front activities discovered that rationing and security measures imposed by both governments changed life at home. Those who explored the big picture of the campaigns of 1942 recognized that the safety of Australia was of paramount importance both to the Australians and to the Americans. The students who had conducted oral histories learned that combat is brutal—no matter who is doing the fighting—and that American GIs stationed in Australia were, for the most part, warmly received by their hosts. Both groups of students came to the conclusion that the alliance between the United States and Australia was critical to the successful waging of the war against Japan.

For the final fifteen minutes, the adults agreed to let the students talk between themselves about life as teenagers in the United States and Australia. There followed a great deal of banter about the television program *Beverly Hills 90210*, music that they listened to, celebrities, fast food, and relationships. This last bit of dialogue put nice closure on a very rewarding experience by all who participated. All the way around it was an exceptional academic adventure.

Conferences with Edward Linenthal and David McCullough

The other two wonderful telephone conferences were held with Ed Linenthal and David McCullough. Ed Linenthal is a professor of history in the Department of Religious Studies at the University of Wisconsin-Oshkosh. He is the author of numerous books on history and public memory, including *Sacred Ground: Americans and Their Battlefields, History Wars: The Enola Gay and Other Battles for the American Past,* and most recently *Preserving Memory: The Struggle to Create America's Holocaust Museum.* Linenthal was the only historian who testified before Congress during the hearings about the National Air and Space Museum's planned exhibit marking the fiftieth anniversary of the United States' bombing of Hiroshima. The exhibit—and the controversy—centered on the *Enola Gay,* the B-29 aircraft from which the bomb was dropped. I had given my students a summer assignment centered on the exhibit and the controversy over the *Enola Gay.* One of the articles in their reading packet was written by Edward Linenthal.

I knew Linenthal's work and decided to see if he would be willing to talk with my students. When I contacted him, he agreed. As soon as school started, we focused on the summer assignment and, in particular, the article by Linenthal. I had each student write a single question he or she would like to ask Linenthal; then I faxed the questions to Linenthal a few days before our arranged conference. I was impressed by how solid my students' historical inquiries were. Some focused on the conflict between "voices" of historical participants and historians themselves. Others explored the potential long-term effects of the controversy over the *Enola Gay* exhibit on other museum exhibits. One student asked, "Do you think in fifty or one hundred years from now that Americans will perceive the dropping of the bombs on Hiroshima and Nagasaki as a moral mistake, or do you think that Americans will look back and see its positive impact on history? How will their views differ from ours now in light of this controversy?"

Linenthal was fantastic with the students. He acknowledged the depth of good questions and recognized the students' ability to think for themselves. To other questions he responded that there are no real easy answers when you get into historical inquiry of this nature. He also indicated that sometimes the best course a historian can take in the pursuit of truth is to recognize that there are often irreconcilable differences.

Again, this strategy was a success for me and my students. And again I was gratified that the students were able to hear about history from a voice with real authority on a particular topic.

The phone conference held with David McCullough was equally success-ful. By the time the class talked with him, I had the technique down to a science. Having the students use note cards for their questions really works, because they have authority over their question: It belongs to them and them alone.

My students know of my admiration for David McCullough and the breadth of his work. I have informed them on many occasions that I look up to David McCullough as a role model, because even though I am an adult, I too need to be inspired if I am going to teach in an engaging and interesting way. They know that I have read all of his books; they are also familiar with his face and voice because he narrates so many of the *American Experience* films I share with my students.

We spoke with McCullough in reference to his first book *The Johnstown Flood,* which is also required summer reading for my Applied History students. I want them to read this because students have often told me that the books they read in other history classes are just plain boring. McCullough's books breathe life. You feel as if you are there when the event is taking place. It's more than a read, it's an experience that I think anybody who loves history should pursue.

Just like the other phone conferences it was a marvelous experi-ence. He too commented on how thoughtful the students' questions were. It's important that the students hear this because it validates them not only as a human beings, but also because someone who is an important authority figure has recognized them as independent thinkers.

I know that a telephone conference is a success when just before I hang up the students give the speaker, whoever it is, a round of applause and, in unison, a sincere "thank-you" and "good-bye." When we debrief as a class after the conference and students comments are in the vein of, "He was really cool!" then I know that an impact has been made.

Some Final Tips

A few tips about guest speakers and conducting telephone conferences:

- Be sure you do your homework and prepare not only yourself but also your students for the experience.

- Make sure that your guest or speaker deals with a topic of relevance to what you are studying—keep the experience within the context of your curriculum.

- When the experience is finished, get back in touch with the people with whom you have worked and let them know not only how much you appreciate their time, but also that for your students it was something meaningful with real merit and value. Regardless of who the person is or what they do, they too are human beings who just as much as you and your students want to be appreciated for their quest or journey in life.

Think about the books or films that have inspired you and your students. Consider contacting the authors or filmmakers by writing to them through their publisher or film production company. In the end, your efforts will pay many dividends for you and your students.

Six

Teaching History Through Film

Good movies make you care, make you believe in possibilities.
                                        Pauline Kael
                                        Going Steady

One day when I was in a video store I happened upon a movie I remembered watching on television as a child. It was Cecil B. DeMille's classic history movie, *The Buccaneer,* about the pirate Jean Laffite, Andrew Jackson, and the battle of New Orleans, and it was for sale—dirt cheap—so I bought it. As I drove home I remembered that this movie—and others like it—had a great deal to do with my falling in love with history. I remember going to the movie theaters to watch movies like *The Robe, How the West Was Won,* and *Major Dundee.* It was in movie theaters that, to a large extent, history became real to me. As I grew older, I began to realize that many of these Hollywood portrayals were historically inaccurate. I was disappointed when I began intensive reading into a particular subject, only to learn that something I had seen on the big screen wasn't true. I learned to be suspicious of Hollywood interpretations of the past.

For better or for worse, much of my initial interest in history was shaped by the film industry. I'm not sure that I would have pursued a career in education had I not been exposed to history through motion pictures. Today, more than ever, our history is being passed on to future generations through an ever-increasing variety of media—be it Hollywood films, television documentaries, or the Internet. I think most historians have recognized this fact and, depending who you read, there are

Figure 6–1
Cartoon by Don Wright, *The Palm Beach Post.*

those who favor what some refer to as history *edutainment* (a blending of learning through a means previously used for entertainment) while others lean to a more conventional, didactic approach to teaching and learning. I think that both have their place in the history classroom.

In the past decade or so, history has found all kinds of new outlets—and debate about these outlets is going strong. Consider the debate over the proposed "Disney's America" theme park near a Civil War battlefield and in the Virginia piedmont. In 1993 the Walt Disney Company announced plans to build a major American History theme park not too far from the nation's capitol. Disney's intent was to present history to visitors in typical Disney fashion using a wealth of technology, much like that used at Disney's EPCOT Center in Orlando, Florida. In addition they would use animatronic figures, like those found at Disney's Hall of Presidents and American Adventure Pavillions, also located in Orlando. Noted scholars and academics lined up on both sides of the issue. Those in favor argued that as long as Disney worked with historical consultants then Disney, with its vision and technical gadgetry, had a right to interpret the past. Those historians opposed to the idea of a history theme park claimed that Disney would not only provide a sanitized version of the past, but that this would be done in a portion of the Virginia piedmont that is sacred, historical ground. In the end Disney backed off under the pressure from a coalition of historians and environmentalists. At the other extreme, Ken Burns' epic film, *The Civil War*, depicted history with skill and care, and it was extremely popular with television viewers. In addition, historically based feature films such as *Gettysburg, Schindler's List, Rosewood,* and *Amistad* have enjoyed popularity—and even some box-office success. Today thousands of young girls learn about early American life by playing with a line of dolls designed to depict different periods of American history, called American Girl Dolls. Thousands of students participate in nationwide extracurricular programs such as Odyssey of the Mind, which may focus on eras or figures from history. In the National History Day competition, students construct their interpretations of the past through display projects, performances, and media presentations.

These changes provide us with many new, rich opportunities for our classes. However, it is our responsibility as educators to teach our students a kind of historical literacy of the marketplace, meaning that they need to be able to distinguish fact from fiction whether they are watching a movie, attending a theme park, or playing with a doll. We also need to use films wisely in our curriculum, making sure that they augment, not control, the curriculum.

Hollywood Goes to School

A number of very good Hollywood films can support any program of instruction in the teaching of U.S. history. I use the films *Glory, Sergeant York, The Best Years of Our Lives, American Graffiti,* and *Modern Times,* but there are many more to choose from. Depending on the film and the amount of time we have, I either use the whole movie or just excerpts. Here is how I use one film.

Real History Versus Reel History

I usually show the film *Glory* at the end of our unit on the Civil War in my U.S. history class. This is a powerful film depicting a story that has long been overlooked by history, that of the first African-American Regiment, the 54th Massachusetts, to be recruited in the North during the Civil War. The movie was both a critical and a commercial success (most students know of it). Clearly, there are historical errors in the film, some of which have drawn sharp criticism from those scholars working in the arena of African-American history. One of *my* problems with this particular film is that it leads viewers to believe that the assault on Fort Wagner in South Carolina was the only significant military engagement that involved the 54th Massachusetts Volunteer Infantry. The film ends with the fort still being held by the Confederates, and in the moments before the credits roll, a paragraph appears on the screen that explains that this regiment's

valor led to increased recognition and acceptance of African Americans in
the Union Army. No mention is made of what happened to the 54th Massachusetts during the rest of the war. So, before I show the film, I point
out this and other inaccuracies to my students. I ask students to be aware
that this film is not a documentary, but rather a producer's or director's
interpretation of the past. Perhaps I should note here that when I show
Glory I use the edited version that was created for the classroom, because
my school district has a policy against showing films that are rated R.

Using a film like *Glory* can lead to all kinds of wonderful discussions
with your students. You can take issue with the fact that the film ignores
entirely the role of two of Frederick Douglass' sons, Lewis and Charles,
who served in the 54th Massachusetts. You can explore the reasons why
director Edward Zwick and his writers might have chosen to leave them
out. Or perhaps you can explore why the film leads viewers to believe
that most of the men who comprised the 54th Massachusetts were
former slaves, when in fact most of the men who served were free blacks
from a number of northern states and Canada. To return to one of my
earlier points, I am compelled to tell students that if the film is shown in a
vacuum we come away with the perception that the assault on Fort Wagner was the only engagement in which the 54th fought. This is not the
case. The largest battle involving the 54th Massachusetts occurred in
1864 in Florida, at the Battle of Olustee. Again, the regiment proved its
mettle as it fought bravely in another Union defeat.

One way that you can assist students in determining for themselves
the difference between real history and reel history in the case of the 54th
Massachusetts is to complement the Hollywood motion picture with one
of the several documentaries that appeared after *Glory* was released. Tri-
Star films, which produced *Glory,* released a documentary, *Glory—The
True Story of Glory Continues,* that uses outtakes from the film to provide
additional historical background on this famous unit. The film is narrated
by Morgan Freeman, one of the stars of *Glory,* and makes an interesting
companion piece. The other film, *The Massachusetts 54th Colored Infantry,*
was produced by filmmaker Jacqueline Shearer for the PBS series, *The
American Experience.* This film is more in the vein of contemporary history
documentary filmmakers as it combines interviews with scholars and
descendants of the men of the 54th, with primary source photographs, to
tell a more complete story. Either film will work if you are seeking to balance the Hollywood interpretation. After you show your students *Glory,*
show them one of these documentaries and ask them to determine what is
actual history and what is Hollywood. You might challenge them by asking
them why and how this story is told from different perspectives, or which
film they feel is more effective in relating the history of this fighting unit.

In general, try to keep these tips in mind for helping students distinguish between real and reel history:

- Give students plenty of background; be sure they understand the historical context in which the story of the movie is taking place.
- Also give students any necessary background information about the political or social climate in which the movie itself was made—for instance, the social climate during which *Glory* was made was very different from the social climate during which *The Birth of a Nation* or *Gone with the Wind* was made.
- Offer students some comparisons between the movie they are watching and others that depict the same story or time period.
- Point out any historical errors, omissions, or embellishments that may affect the way students perceive the events in the movie.

Use Excerpts

Another way to use feature length films in class is to use certain scenes from a motion picture to make a particular point. Suppose that you are covering the Civil Rights movement. Scenes from many films available in videotape format can support your curriculum. You might want to consider using excerpts from *The Long Walk Home*, about the Montgomery Bus Boycott, or *Crisis at Central High*, a docudrama about the Little Rock, Arkansas, School Crisis in 1957. Many of these films star actors and actresses that students can relate to and this helps give the film and its story a particular dimension because your students can personally link themselves to the movie.

Combine Activities

One way that I dovetail films with other parts of my curriculum to help support my instructional objectives is to combine elements of film with other published lesson plan activities, such as the Teaching with Historic Places materials that were discussed in Chapter 2. Combining elements from the movie *Tora, Tora, Tora* with the lesson plan on the *U.S.S. Arizona Memorial*, written by National Park Service Ranger John Vierra, who worked at the *Arizona Memorial*, is very effective. It engages the senses and thus multiple intelligences. In addition, every kind of learning style is addressed when you present material in this fashion. Students look at old photos, read maps, examine written primary source material, and then watch the scene from the movie where the Arizona is sunk. An excellent follow-up is to show students the film clips of President Franklin Roosevelt delivering his War Address to Congress the day after the December 7 attack on Pearl Harbor. All of this makes history come alive for the students.

Create Your Own Film Festival

Another effective way to use film is to create your own film festival. I do this for my U.S. history classes. Films can be an excellent teaching tool provided they don't consume your curriculum. I learned this the hard way the first year I tried it. However, there are some films that I think students should be exposed to because they are classics and because the students may not have another chance to see them. So I created a film festival.

When I first set out to design the film festival, I was seeking to bring together much of the twentieth century as seen through film. I wanted one film to represent each of the decades, from the 1930s to the 1960s. I thought long and hard about what films to use. For the 1930s, I chose Charlie Chaplin's classic comedy, *Modern Times*. To cover American entry into World War II, I relied on Gary Cooper and his dynamic performance in *Sergeant York*. Though this film is a story set during World War I, it was produced on the eve of American entry into World War II in 1940; in some ways it is a propaganda piece used to urge American preparation for entry into the Second World War. For post–World War II America, I decided to use *The Best Years of Our Lives*. After some initial nervousness, because I thought that the story line might bore my students, I discovered to my delight that my students loved this movie. To cover the 1950s and early 1960s, I decided to use George Lucas' *American Graffiti*. I also used the 1951 science fiction classic *The Day the Earth Stood Still* and Stanley Kubrick's *Dr. Strangelove* to cover the Cold War, but neither of these films was successful with my students so I dropped them from the lineup and opted not to use a film to cover the Cold War.

I felt comfortable showing these films to my classes after I had done the necessary background reading and research I needed to do for each film. You might ask what about the Vietnam Era? Why haven't I included films like *The Deer Hunter, Apocalypse Now,* or *Platoon?* Clearly these are good films and they would assist a teacher in covering the American experience in Vietnam, but they are not approved by my school system because of the R rating.

As I mentioned, the first year I tried to cram all the movies into class time, which was a disaster. The films chewed up too much time. So the second year, I began to show the films after school one day a week and gave students the option of picking one film to watch. The only exception to this was the film *The Best Years of Our Lives,* which I chose to show to all of my students. They loved it. They saw this as a very human film that was rooted in a reality with which many of them could identify. Based on their reaction I decided to show the film to my classes in its entirety.

Developing Visual Literacy

Watching movies in my class is not a *freebie*. There are activities connected with just about everything we watch. I'm interested in my students being active learners as they watch a film unfold—they are not, under any circumstances, to be passive receptacles. It is imperative with today's students, given how much visual stimuli they are exposed to, that we as educators help facilitate the development of their visual literacy. Some film activities are as simple as answering questions on a worksheet. These questions generally are connected to content and usually lead students to identify the main points of a film. Using the Historical Head format, mentioned earlier, demands that students use higher-level thinking skills to decide for themselves what is important. For the film festival I focused not only on objectives connected to visual literacy, but also on writing and researching skills connected to watching these films. After having watched their film of choice, students are assigned a question that they must answer in a multipage research project. The questions, tied directly to the films, revolve around how the motion picture mirrors the time period depicted in the film. I provide students with a thesis question that they are to work on. For *Modern Times* and *The Best Years of Our Lives* the question reads: "How do these motion pictures mirror and reflect the times as demonstrated in the motion picture?" The question for *Sergeant York* has more to do with the war-preparedness movement in the United States in 1940 and reads: "How does the motion picture *Sergeant York* illustrate the beliefs on the part of some Americans, that the United States should be actively preparing for war in 1940?" For *American Graffiti*, I ask students to examine how this film reflects the last moment of innocence in the United States before the turbulence in the 1960s over Vietnam and a changing national and social political agenda.

As part of their assignment, students are required to conduct and document within their papers an oral history from someone who experienced the various eras. I tell students to consider interviewing parents and grandparents or aunts and uncles. Students have been directed to the local VFW or American Legion posts to interview veterans of World War II. Some students even surf the Internet looking for ideas to add to their papers. I direct the students to discuss at least three scenes from each film as part of the support in their papers. For each scene there has to be solid discussion with documented support from historical reality. Again, let me draw from the film *The Best Years of Our Lives*. Following are three potential scenes or themes students might consider when writing their papers:

- One of the characters, Homer Parrish—played by double amputee Harold Russell, who received an Oscar for Best Supporting Actor—has to learn to adjust to life at home without use of his hands. One of the subplots of the film deals with this problem and dilemma faced not only by Homer, but also by those who love him.

- The second character, Fred Stevens—played by actor Frederick March, who also earned an Oscar for Best Actor—has to contend with alcoholism.
- The third subplot deals with Fred Derry, played by Dana Andrews, as he tries to hold down a job and deal with a wife who married him strictly for his uniform.

I ask the students to consider using these images or ideas to develop their papers. When showing these films, I sometimes put the VCR on pause at critical scenes, so that I can discuss them more deeply with my students. A scene from *The Best Years of Our Lives* that I find particularly powerful is the scene where Fred walks through a scrap yard of obsolete bombers, the kind of aircraft in which he served as a bombardier. I ask students to consider finding out about what happened to war material after the war and how they might relate their findings to this particular film image.

After the papers are turned in for evaluation, I ask students to respond in their journals and talk about their interview experiences or oral histories. I remember one particular student who, for the movie *The Best Years of Our Lives,* interviewed her grandfather who served in Europe during World War II. She wrote that the interview helped her to understand her grandfather, who before had never really talked about his war experiences. The student recorded that for her, the school assignment turned into a greater lesson about her own identity and roots. She not only mastered the intellectual objectives I had established, but also was able to sense her own family's place in the course of American history. Other students find it somewhat interesting that some of their parents were part of the hippie and peace movement during the Vietnam War.

When you assign a project like this, you need to talk about each movie before and after the film is shown. Briefly discuss with your students the plot or themes of each film and which characters or scenes are of importance. The movies have to be set in their proper historical context. You will find that some students need more help than others, particularly in learning about how they might interview people who experienced the actual history. Some of your stronger students might be able to take off and run with the assignment, but others will need support.

Even though *The Best Years of Our Lives* is a personal favorite, most of my students for the Film Festival research assignment gravitate toward *American Graffiti.* I think the students see themselves mirrored in the characters in this movie more than in any other film. While on the surface the movie might seem like an obvious choice for students to research and write about, at a very deep level they come to understand that in many ways they aren't that far removed from the history of a generation and a half ago.

Past Imperfect

If you are interested in pursuing using "history type movies" in your academic program, I would strongly suggest that you review the 1995 publication *Past Imperfect: History According to the Movies*, edited by Mark C. Carnes. This book makes an excellent teacher resource. It contains essays written by leading scholars who are experts in their fields on sixty Hollywood films about historical genres, some of which are mentioned in this chapter. The writers include James McPherson, Stephen Ambrose, Geoffrey C. Ward, and William Manchester, among others. The essays are short but insightful and go a long way toward clearing up any historical misconceptions created by the films. In an excellent opening to the book—"A Conversation Between Eric Foner and John Sayles"—the scholar (Foner) and the filmmaker (Sayles) discuss the problems and issues faced by those who create history films and those who critique them. It is reading that makes solid food for thought because it is imperative if you use Hollywood films to teach about history that you clarify for students what is fact and what is fiction. Students need to be informed that like any art form, film is someone's interpretation of the past, and that they need to watch the film with a healthy dose of skepticism. Walter Cronkite in his recent publication *A Reporter's Life* addresses this issue:

> It is generally accepted that movies built on novels depicting ancient history beyond the reach of this generation's researchers for the most part reflect their producer's interpretation of the past and cannot be viewed otherwise. But any so-called docudramas produced in times contemporary with the events they pretend to depict must be suspect. It is a dangerous cinematic form. Present and future generations are likely to assume that the film reflects thorough, factual, journalistic reporting of current events. They are likely to ignore that the idea of the film is only the producer's interpretation of events—an interpretation that is frequently afflicted with paid propaganda, special pleading or commercial theatrical hype. It is a great way to distort, and a very poor way to teach, history.

At the conclusion of showing a Hollywood history film, I have students take out a sheet of notepaper, dividing it in half with a pen to create two columns, one labeled History, the other coloumn labeled Hollywood. Then, depending on resource material available, I ask them to place in the proper column the things that were actual history and the things that were Hollywood's embellishment. I find satisfaction in knowing that at least I helped keep the record straight.

Using History Documentaries

Never before in the history of the media has there been such a proliferation of historical documentaries. This is a boon to history teachers. These films can also help you build your curriculum if you preview them. As with the feature films, the use of documentaries must not direct your curriculum, but rather be shaped by your objectives and what you want your students to learn. Again, my students know that whenever I show a film, some exercise or activity will be tied to it. I want my students to think about, analyze, and synthesize information that they have extracted from whatever film we are watching.

The American Experience

I'd like to state at the outset that I think that there is no finer program available to history educators today than the *The American Experience* series that is broadcast on PBS. I have found these films extremely useful in helping my students understand the complexity of American history. Most of the films are well balanced, present the views of a variety of noted historians, and are graphically compelling. What I most like about the series is that over the years it has touched on just about every aspect of American history—science, business, entertainment, racial issues, politics, and America at war to name a few. As well, the series is not afraid of confronting historical issues head on.

The educational outreach staff at PBS have created lesson plans that accompany just about every film. They can be obtained by contacting your local PBS affiliate, provided they air *The American Experience*. I have found these to be well written and useful in the classroom.

For my own assignments I like to use the Historical Head activity and student journal writing, both discussed in Chapter 1, when using documentaries. My students also seem to like this approach. Using these strategies forces students to focus on the content of the film while not having to worry about getting caught up in the minutiae of detail. I want them to see the "big picture" and how the topic of the film is tied to the context of American history. For example, the film *Frederick Douglass: When the Lion Wrote History* chronicles the span of Douglass' remarkable life and allows the students to reflect on the various contributions Douglass made to the United States as well as to consider his struggle and the struggle of African Americans in the nineteenth century. For this particular film I ask students to write in their journals about the subtitle of the documentary to explain the idea of what is meant by the phrase, *When the Lion Wrote History*. Some students like to compare the title of the film to Douglass' physical features, most notably how he appeared to have a mane around his head. Other students discuss Douglass' powerful voice and how as a spokesperson for Black Americans Douglass took the lead in articulating the concerns of the Black community. Other students interpret Douglass as being the most influential African American of the nineteenth century, and that by his presence and actions he helped shape history, thereby helping to write it.

Another excellent title from the series is the film *Ida B. Wells: A Passion for Justice*, for which I also use the Historical Head and journal technique. The reason I really like to use this film is that it makes students angry. This film communicates the absolute terror that some African Americans endured only one hundred years ago, and the visual imagery is both chilling and compelling. Most students have never heard of Ida B. Wells-Barnett before. She is overlooked in textbooks, yet she was a major advocate for the rights of African Americans toward the close of the nineteenth century, particularly in her scathing editorials about the plague of lynchings that swept the United States a century ago. After I show this film, students are really charged up because the story of Wells and her crusade to end this dark period in American history is so powerful. They get into writing in their journals, and when we discuss what they wrote they share their strong opinions about the injustices endured by Black Americans. Many of them, even African-American students, freely admit that they never knew about the life of Wells-Barnett.

Other films from *The American Experience* that work well with students are *The Donner Party*, and the film about the Indian Boarding School program, *In the White Man's Image*. I attribute the success of these films to their ability to tell stories in a way that touches the human soul and spirit. In essence, *The American Experience* series has the capacity to be haunting yet very real.

For most of these films I show the entire program, which generally runs about 55 minutes. Occasionally I will stop and pause the film to highlight or discuss a particular point I want the students to understand. In doing so, this helps me let them know what I want them to learn from the experience. Students have told me that they find this approach to showing films helpful.

Longer Documentaries

What about the longer documentary programs such as Ken Burns' *Civil War* or his epic on baseball? How can a teacher effectively use these films without taking up an inordinate amount of class time? For these films I use selected segments to illustrate a particular theme or idea. When I use the *Civil War* series, I like to tie parts of episodes to particular primary source documents. While the program is a masterpiece, some segments are more powerful than others. Segments I have used over the years include the coverage on the Battle of Antietam, the examination of the

Battle of Gettysburg, and the material related to Sherman's March to the Sea. All are equally compelling, but let's explore the use of Sherman's March to the Sea, which is part of the episode called "War Is All Hell." I use the narrative about Sherman's March to the Sea in conjunction with the accounts of four individuals who experienced this event in history. First I show the video to introduce the subject, then after the video I provide students some primary source readings connected with the March to the Sea. These primary accounts, which can be found in any good narrative about Sherman's March, include a northern soldier's perspective, two views of southern women who saw their property destroyed, and a letter from Sherman to the mayor and members of the city council of Atlanta, which expresses his position regarding his actions. I use this combined viewing and reading activity to lead students into a discussion about the justification of Sherman's infamous orders to "Make Georgia Howl." Then I read to students from Jerry Ellis' *Marching Through Georgia: My Walk with Sherman*. Ellis—whose publicist has called him an inveterate traveler, storyteller, and adventurer—writes about his walking various historic trails including the Cherokee Trail of Tears and the Pony Express route; he has a gift for making the past become relevant to the present. His musings are always thoughtful and insightful, and sharing his writings with my students has become one of my favorite activities. Much of Ellis' writing is based on the conversations with people he meets as he walks or rides along some actual pathway of the past. Below is a passage from *Marching Through Georgia* that always helps my students build connections between the past and the present.

> While Bud and I speed down the Georgia highway, I find myself studying him from the corner of my eye. I wish I could see deeply enough into his soul to grasp all that he thinks and feels about being a Southerner and a descendant of Confederate soldiers who were victims of the March to the Sea.
>
> "What are your thoughts on Sherman?" I ask, once again amazing myself with my discreet and subtle investigative style.
>
> "Well, I don't like revisionist history," Bud begins. "I think to really love history you have to look at it in the context of the times. In his time Sherman was something people had never seen before. If you look at him through the eyes of today, he seems pretty mild. He moved through enemy territory and didn't slaughter men, women, and children. His burning had some sort of rhyme and reason, so some people think what's the big deal? But Colonel Raines offered Lee a land mine he had developed and Lee turned it down. He said, 'I will not make war on noncombatants.' I mean, Lee wouldn't even consider it."
>
> "If you look at what Sherman did from that perspective he's a big pill to swallow. After we've been through Cambodia, Bosnia, and the Holocaust, Sherman might not seem like that much. But when you go back to 1864, to a small hamlet like Milledgeville, and 30,000 soldiers

with 5,000 teamsters and wagons storm in and leave families scratching the dirt in the heart of winter hoping to find a little cornmeal or something to feed themselves and their children, then you don't exactly have the prettiest picture in the world. I just don't think you can look at history with today's values and reinterpret it to suit your own outlook. You have to think about Sherman the way people in his own lifetime did."

"I'm not a person flash-frozen in 1865 who walks around mumbling out of the side of his mouth *if only the South had won The War,* as my grandmother always called it. No, I even have some admiration for Sherman's strategy. This was the breadbasket of the South. But he didn't have to destroy all the food, because the railroads were being wrecked and there was no way to get supplies to Confederates after he left. With all the people moving into Georgia now, I suspect in time all this will just be a footnote in history anyway."

In combining the film segments, the primary source readings, and the selection from Ellis' book I can demonstrate to students the timeless quality of history. This is just one of many ways that you can adapt various elements of film and motion picture in your classes without feeling guilty for using precious class time. It can be an effective way of pulling much of what your students are studying together.

An Applied History Unit on Film and Interpretation

So far, I have talked about using film in my standard U.S. history curriculum. Now I would like to share with you how film is used in the Applied History class. I call the unit "History Through Film and Fiction: What's the Truth?" This unit of study is based on two historical events and how they have been depicted both in Hollywood motion pictures and in documentaries. The two events we examine are the Battle of Gettysburg and the Allied Invasion of Normandy. Films that are incorporated into the unit include Ron Maxwell's *Gettysburg,* which I show in its entirety even though it's four hours long. Since Applied History is offered the last period of the day I start the film right as class begins and the students continue watching the movie after school is dismissed. I also use selected scenes from Daryl F. Zanuck's *The Longest Day,* which deal exclusively with American participation on D-Day (June 6, 1944).

Finally, I include documentary filmmaker Charles Guggenheim's Fiftieth Anniversary documentary, *D-Day* , which appeared on *The American Experience* and is the official film of the planned D-Day National Museum in New Orleans. For selected readings I use portions of Cornelius Ryan's book *The Longest Day,* Michael Shaara's classic Civil War novel, *The Killer Angels,* and Joshua Lawrence Chamberlain's account of the stand of the 20th Maine on Little Round Top during the Battle of Gettysburg. Students

Figure 6–2
Guest speaker Brian Pohanka talks about when "History Meets Hollywood."

also may opt to read the account of William C. Oates, Colonel of the 15th Alabama Regiment that fought against Chamberlain's men from Maine on Little Round Top. Students also read the "Conversation Between Eric Foner and John Sayles" mentioned earlier and historian Stephen Ambrose's essay on *The Longest Day,* which can be found in *Past Imperfect.* Finally, students read an assortment of oral history accounts from D-Day veterans who are still alive—most notably men from the rural Virginia community of Bedford, a community which lost more men on D-Day than any other community in the United States. My teaching this unit combines not only the films and readings, but also site-specific slides I have shot at Gettysburg, in Normandy, and in the town of Bedford. We also undertake a daylong visit to Gettysburg and to Bedford to meet and talk with the men from Company A of the 29th Infantry Division, which went ashore in the first wave at Omaha Beach. In addition, Civil War historian, Brian Pohanka, who was the history consultant for the motion pictures *Glory* and *Gettysburg,* comes in and speaks to my students about what happens when "History Meets Hollywood."

Before we start the three-week unit, I provide students with a work plan as well as the questions that they are to answer based on their exposure to all of the elements just discussed. They are required to utilize the films, their readings, and their field trip experiences to answer the following questions:

1. Given historical films, books, and novels, which medium affords greater latitude for the interpretation of historical events and what are the tools that both authors and filmmakers employ in their interpretation of those events?

2. In addition, what responsibilities do you have as a critical reviewer and reader when you view history films or read historical fiction?

3. Given the entertainment aspect of film, fiction, and good narrative history, can they be valid interpretations of the past? Why and how? (I think this is a question that they've never considered before, though most of them, by the time they turn in their papers, have done a good job wrestling with the issue.)

One student commented, ". . . filmmakers of all sorts find that history is a rich source of inspiration for their works. However, such creative minds sometime find it difficult to resist the temptation to change historical details to make their work colorful, dramatic or entertaining. . . . Given the added elements of sight and sound filmmakers have more freedom in interpreting historical events, and the public has a greater chance of learning false history."

Another student argued her case from a rather interdisciplinary approach,

> In geometry, a transverse line is a line that cuts through another line in such a way that divides the second in two angles. By laws of geometry, the sum of these angles will always equal one hundred eighty degrees. Perhaps in a society's analysis of its historical mediums, a moment should be given to the laws of geometry. Movies, books, television documentaries, and museum exhibitions are the topic of much controversy when the transverse line is faintly delineated between what is portrayed as reality and what is depicted as fiction. Before one can adequately judge the accuracy of the historical content presented, it is important to consider the purpose of these genres: is a movie produced to educate or entertain? For money or ratings? Is a documentary aired for purposes of

persuasion or does the filmmaker have other motives? In an effort to afford the greater latitude for interpretations, these mediums complement each other in a way that fulfills each of the purposes outlined above. Therefore, it is the responsibility of the viewer to recognize such purposes, regard the presented information with respect to these goals, and to supplement opinion, fact, or fiction with the textbook. When delineated, movies and novels ideally work in such a way that when the reader finishes his research, he is not left with one angle, but with two, the sum of which equals a completed and accurate depiction of a historical event . . . If movies and books were placed on a geometric plane and a vertical line drawn through the midpoint at any possible angle, one resultant angle would be labeled movies, the other books. Both angles together produce the completed equation; they must be complementary. The remaining angle is what Hollywood audiences are missing when they view historical films; they must remember that everything one sees cannot be taken at face value.

The use of film can be a powerful tool in helping you make history more alive, authentic, and vibrant. If employed with care in the classroom, motion pictures can strengthen your program, while helping you develop in your students solid historical- and critical-thinking skills in addition to visual literacy.

I would also recommend that you turn to some of the work by Ron Briley, a history teacher at Sandia Prepatory School in Albuquerque, New Mexico. Briley has pioneered the use of film media in his history classes and written extensively about film as a teaching tool in a number of professional journals. His research stands as the benchmark for this particular technique in the teaching of history.

Here are some final thoughts for you to consider in preparing lessons based on film resources.

- Be sure to preview all material. Edit out portions of the film that are not relevant to your objectives for your students.

- Read the actual history of the account you are showing through film, so that you can help your students know what actually happened.

- Be certain to advise your classes that any film is a form of art in which the filmmaker is trying to manipulate them to feel or think something. This will give them good food for thought.

- Always be certain that using film complements your curriculum but does not consume it.

As to that film that I ended up purchasing at the video store, well, even though I now know the real story of the battle of New Orleans, I still can't help but recall that one night when as a child I was swept away into the past by what I saw on TV.

Seven

Doing History
Applied History and Interning

The past is never dead.

William Faulkner
Requiem for a Nun

Genesis

By now you know that my approach to teaching history is very tactile and engaging to the senses. In Chapter 1 I touched upon some of the basic elements of the Applied History class. Here I'd like to provide a more detailed look at this unique class and present some ideas to help you think about launching a similar course at your school.

My experience as the recipient of a grant funded by the National Endowment of the Humanities and the Council for Basic Education had been a transforming experience. I had had a chance to conduct research in archival repositories and at several historic sites. Working as a scholar and gathering information rather than teaching it had jump-started my intellectual battery and I was ready to take on new horizons.

How wonderful would it be for students to experience the same kinds of things—to touch the past in a way that only few (sadly, too few) professionals know. I wanted to create an atmosphere that permitted students to engage history directly. We've all seen signs at museums or historic sites that read "Do Not Touch." Well, I wanted my students to be able to touch. It was with this in mind that I built the Applied History class.

In the two years that it took to design the class I talked with a great many professionals inside education and public history circles. I went to a number of institutions soliciting and canvassing their opinion. Fortunately, the concept of the course was approved by the Social Studies specialists of Fairfax County Public Schools. Two key institutional allies proved to be Sherry Birk, the Curator of Prints and Drawings for the American Institute of Architecture Foundation, and Mary Dyer, Coordinator of Internships and Fellowships at the Smithsonian Institutions National Museum of American History. I had met both women during my Summer Independent Study Fellowship. One of my concerns at the time was whether or not institutions such as the Smithsonian would scoff at the idea of working with high school students. But Dyer was very adamant in saying that she could arrange internships within the museum for any kind of person with any kind of interest. She explained that even if I had a student, who might appear on the outside to be a kind of rough character, but who liked to work with automobiles, that she could arrange for that student to work with his interests on any number of motorized vehicles that are in the museum's collection. Conversely, she said that if I had a student who liked or played a fine musical instrument, such as a violin, she could place that student with a curator who oversees the museum's collection of historical musical instruments.

And so began the intense preparation and groundwork necessary for laying out the objectives and design of the course. It was also fortuitous that at this time within the museum community and public history sites or agencies recognition had developed of the value of working with schools, at the secondary level, in a more direct way. My timing could not have been more opportune.

Creating an Applied History Class

No matter where you live and work, there are bound to be historic sites, historical societies, archival repositories, museums, or history agencies in your neighborhood that serve your community by keeping a record of the past. The staff that work at these places are always looking for help in the form of volunteers to assist them with the site or museum's mission. These individuals usually love to share information about their site with anyone who is interested.

Basic Tips

Here are a few basic tips for creating an Applied History course.

1. Be confident in your ability as a salesman to sell not only yourself, but your vision and program as well.

2. Get your thoughts down on paper and be prepared to make as many formal presentations as necessary. At one point I ended up meeting with all of the curators of the museum properties in Alexandria, Virginia, at one of their monthly meetings. I had prepared handouts that included my objectives as well as the learning objectives that I outlined for my students. I also took with me the needed ammunition of saying that the National Museum of American History had come on board with me. It worked: A number of the curators expressed a desire to work with the program.

3. Visit the sites or museums that you are interested in working with to get a sense of each place.

4. Find out if potential sites or museums have Curators of Education on their staffs and contact them. See if you can meet with them and talk with them about your ideas. Find out if they have any educational outreach or extension programs. If they do, see if you can work with them in creating an internship.

5. Review the professional literature, particularly articles concerning student service programs. At the time I was creating Applied History not much material was available; today the notion of student service programs for school credit is widely practiced.

6. Don't get frustrated if some museums or historic sites refuse to take up your offer. You will find that most places will be willing to give this a try.

Once I had internship sponsors lined up, I took the program of studies that I had created, along with all my notes and information, presented them to my principal, who forwarded them to the school division Office of Instruction where the course was approved. They were persuaded by the innovative nature of the program and its rigorous academic agenda.

Once I knew that the class had been approved I began to visit all of the eleventh-grade U.S. history classes at West Springfield. I conducted a ten-minute presentation to each class explaining and outlining the course. When the students finished their course selection process later that spring, more than fifty students had enrolled for Applied History.

Selecting the Class

I would suspect that at any school a course like this would be popular among students. You will be surprised at how many students in your school *really like* history. Since the class size had been capped at twenty-five, this meant I needed to cut that number in half. For this purpose a screening process was put in place. My department chair and I came up with a questionnaire that consisted of some short answer questions that demonstrated the high standards I had outlined for the class. These included:

- What kinds of skills and enthusiasms can you contribute to this class?
- Are you willing to participate in field trip experiences on the weekend?
- Can you provide your own transportation to and from your internship site?
- Are you willing to commit to five hours a week or 100 hours of service time during the second semester at your internship site?
- Are you willing to act and dress as a professional at your internship?
- Are you willing to have your work evaluated and assessed by Mr. Percoco and your cooperating sponsor?
- What kinds of things in history are an interest to you?

One of my most important criteria was to select students who had a sincere interest in history, but who also would be responsible and mature enough to complete the necessary five hours a week internship requirement. It would be during the second semester that these students would receive early release time to leave school and work at their internships. A model in the school system for internship-based programs had been established with a Political Science course. Students had to work a minimum of five hours a week to satisfy the requirements. Consequently, the class had to meet the last period of the day.

Even though high standards for the course were set, I didn't want to discourage students from signing up. In particular I did not want students who had a learning disability to feel that they wouldn't have a shot at being selected. When I make my final selections, I am careful to include students with a variety of learning styles and personalities in the final number. I also like to have a diversified population based on gender, race, and culture. Bringing together this cross section of students creates a more dynamic learning environment. Within our special community we can study different points of views and explore cultural biases.

The questionnaires were evaluated by myself and my department chair. I had also asked for input from my colleagues in the department about whether or not they would recommend a particular student.

The first year of the course involved a great deal of trial and error. Even though I had formulated the curriculum on paper, it still needed to be worked out in practice. To be sure, we had some rough moments. I removed one student from the program because of immaturity exhibited during the classroom phase that carried over to his internship. I also learned that a time sheet was needed for each student to keep track of their hours. Some of the internship sites were better prepared to handle student internships than others, and some used the students to do extended clerical work, which was not my intent. For all of us, it was a real learning experience. Overall the program's framework has remained the same since 1991. The changes made since then were based mostly on those problems that emerged during the first year. Most of the internship sites have stayed with the program. Each year I know these sites will provide students with exceptional learning opportunities; a number of sites have sponsored one or more interns every year since the course's inception. Each year I also look for new possibilities for the students; in some instances, I have been contacted by a museum or agency, which has heard about the program through word of mouth, and would like to become involved. Other times I have released students from a program that didn't measure up to the standards I have established. This is not an easy thing to do, but it is imperative if the program is going to have merit and credibility.

I do not personally place students at their internships. Rather during the months of December and early January, the various sponsors come and speak to my classes about their site, property, or agency. The sponsors—usually the site's educational curator—present their programs and project possibilities to the students. Many offer a slide program and provide students with handouts or brochures about their site. They also explain the particular mission of their site or museum so that the students can understand the organization's historical context. Additionally, most sites now have web pages. Students can access the website to glean additional information about the site, if they so desire. After the speaker series, the students decide where they would like to work.

One of the things that I think is a plus about the internships is that very few of them are connected with military history. Much of the focus of the first semester is centered around military history, and the internships provide students a solid place to work in social or political history. The types of internships available have a much broader appeal and reflect the diversity of opportunities available in a public history setting. Most of the cooperating sites or museums provide students with a placement under their office of volunteers. In some cases students receive parking privileges or other perks associated with their sites.

Since 1991 students have worked as archeologists both in the lab and in the field; others have worked as interpreters of living history, while some have chosen to work in collections management or historic preservation; and some have become docents, giving tours at their site. In all cases students have come away with a much greater appreciation of the role of history in society as well as with an understanding of a variety of working options in the field of history.

The Antietam National Battlefield Memorial Illumination

Increasingly in the literature there is an emphasis on generating student service programs. The Applied History class has increasingly moved down this avenue. Our work each December on the outskirts of Sharpsburg, Maryland, helps me meet one of my most important goals, that of giving service to an organization in the present, while at the same time returning a debt to those generations before us. It is of no coincidence that the last field trip before the internship phase of the course begins is our class participation in the annual Antietam National Battlefield Memorial Illumination. Begun in 1989, this annual program is an effort to remember in a significant and poignant way the 23,110 Americans who fell September 17, 1862, on the battlefield along the Antietam Creek near Sharpsburg, Maryland. The program requires eight hundred volunteers to place 23,110 votive candles on the battlefield, during the daylight hours of the first Saturday in December, which they then light. After the candles are lit and the sun goes down, the battlefield is opened up for visitors who can drive through the park. So many visitors come to this event each year that people wait for hours to drive through.

When I first decided to have the class participate in this activity, I thought that it would be another field trip connected to remembering the past in an unusual way. However, the importance of the volunteer aspect of the experience, which is coordinated by local business woman, Georgene Charles, has added a dimension to the Applied History class course that I had never even considered—volunteerism and service. The Antietam Illumination is somewhat different from other field trips because here the students have to give something back to the past. They actively participate in every step of the process. Placing the seven hundred votive candles that each volunteer is responsible for is a long, tedious job. It must be done correctly, and it takes several hours.

After the candles are lit, all of the volunteers meet at the Maryland State Monument where a special ceremony is held. As the sun goes down and the lighted candles begin to glow, the volunteers listen to gospel and freedom songs sung by an African-American Baptist choir as well as to a lone bagpiper, dressed in period clothing, play "Amazing Grace" and "Going Home." Speakers include top officials from the National Park Service, historians, and individuals involved in the forefront of Civil War site preservation. They speak not only about the battle and the men who fell that terrible September day in 1862, but also about how an event of this size and magnitude could not take place without the hundreds of volunteers who make it possible. After the ceremony, the volunteers are given the first place in the long line of cars to pay tribute through the

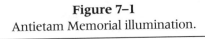

Figure 7–1
Antietam Memorial illumination.

night to those who fell on the bloodiest day in American history. As we make our way along the five-mile journey, I often hear students respond to this experience as being *awesome*. Just when you think that there can be no more candles, you crest a hill and see the flickers of thousands of more candles crossing the rolling Maryland countryside. In a very real and meaningful way, everyone who participates in this event can truly appreciate how many fell when they see all those 23,110 candles flickering in the dark. These students, in their action of remembrance, confront history in a deeply personal and spiritual way. We have participated in a consecration.

As is my custom, I ask students to write in their journals about their experiences, reflecting on their role as volunteers and what the day meant to them. One sensitive student wrote:

> 23,110 soldiers fell at Antietam Battlefield. It was the bloodiest day in American history. I always knew the statistics, but the 23,110 casualties never really came home to me until I rode over that first hill and saw lights stretching in every direction as far as I could see.
>
> It was not an easy day, as far as putting out the votive candles. But as I worked, my entire body telling me to get back in the car and put the heat on, I began to think of those soldiers who those paper bags represented. They had a much harder job to do than I did, and I'll bet they didn't have fur-lined gloves.

On the way to the battlefield, my father insisted on playing his *Civil War* tape, from the Ken Burns PBS film. At the end of the tape is Sullivan Ballou's letter to his wife Sarah. As I began to light the candles for all the men who fell where I was standing over one hundred thirty years ago, I thought of Ballou's letter, and suddenly each candle I lit began to have a name, a face. I wondered who these people had been, and what kind of lives they had led before war tore them apart. How might our nation's history have been changed had just one of those men who had died, lived to make his contribution to the world? What never happened because of Antietam? How much more than lives was lost there?

I was rhythmically lighting candles, when suddenly, not ten feet from me, a bag caught fire and burst into flames. I was so lost in my thoughts that I jumped about ten feet. I stared hard at that burning bag for a long time. Cannon fire? A fallen angel? A ghost on the battlefield making his presence known? Throughout the night, bags would abruptly catch fire, making them stand out in one brief, final blaze of glory. In a way, these burning bags had almost a greater impact on me than the rows and rows of candles. It made the battlefield seem more real, somehow. With each dying candle, one more soldier was dying; his name to be forgotten over time. I wonder if, while he was closing his eyes for the last time, he saw a small fire slowly dying out into the blackness of night?

I stood at the Maryland memorial and looked out over the battlefield. The sun was going down, and slowly the thousands of candles began to glow to life. It was beautiful, and I felt guilty for thinking of it as such. What happened at Antietam was not beautiful or spiritual or glorious. It was war, a war that left scars which have yet to heal in our country. And that's what had to be remembered as I looked out over the fields.

Jumping into the Fray: Internship Stories

It is a real joy to watch my Applied History students grow over the relatively short period that they work as interns. A number of students have had such successful experiences that they have continued with their particular interest into college and beyond. During an internship, I visit each student at least twice over the course of the internship and am constantly amazed at how quickly they mesh with the program with which they are working. I think that this is in part because they select for themselves where they want to work, and thereby let their interests carry them forward. Mostly, when I visit the students, I let them do the talking as they explain the details of the various projects on which they are working. In their own right they have become experts, now assuming the role of teacher and explaining to me what they are doing and why they are doing it. Some vignettes of the experiences student interns have had working with history out in the field follow.

One year a student helped restore a mid–nineteenth century farm quilt at the National Museum of American History. Seated behind a conservation table, wearing white lab gloves, in one of the institution's conservation labs, she spoke eloquently about how she and the curator first had to clean the quilt using special chemicals and then to frame out the quilt on the table where she was repairing holes in the fabric. She was very much at home.

Another student—who also worked at the National Museum of American History, but in the political history division—was on hand when a very special package arrived containing material that would become part of the museum's permanent collection. H. Ross Perot had donated the props that he used during his infomercials for the 1992 Presidential Campaign to the museum. The props included his charts and his armadillo pointer. On the day that I visited with the young man who worked in this area of the museum, he was directed by his supervising curator to unpack Perot's props. For him, as for me, history suddenly had a very relevant face, and we discussed how everything, be it an object, a document, or a person, somehow becomes a part of history.

Two other students who also worked at the Museum of American History spent their four-month internship helping to prepare the Science and American Life Exhibit. These two students conducted relevant research at the Library of Congress and also photographed objects from the exhibit that were to be displayed in the exhibition catalogue. By working in this particular capacity they were able to tap not only their interest in history, but they were also able to make the connection that history is tied to other disciplines, in their case, science. This is how my objective of having students embrace history in a direct way becomes reality. Perhaps that is what makes all of these internships so important— whether students work at the Museum of American History or at a historic house site or smaller museum, they get to make the significant connection between history and life. They find history everywhere!

The students who have worked with Sherry Birk at the Octagon Museum always have fascinating projects to work on. These experiences are made doubly wonderful because of Birk's commitment to my ideas and goals. She has an ability to create projects that are meaningful not only for her institution, but also for the interns. For her, students have worked in collections management, exhibit installation, curatorial accessioning, and historic preservation. In each case, the students have come away from their experience under her mentorship with new perspectives about how we care for and treat the past. The internships at the Octagon are also very hands-on historical experiences.

The Octagon House was one of the first houses to be built shortly after Washington, D.C.—then called Federal City—was laid out. The original owner, John Tayloe, was a friend of George Washington's.

Washington convinced him to build his residence not too far from the President's mansion. The house derives its name from its unusual design. William Thornton, first Architect of the United States Capitol, and one of America's premier early architects, designed Tayloe's residence. Today, the Octagon, managed by the American Institute of Architects, serves not only as a historic house museum, but also as a gallery for various art shows and exhibitions. One year as part of the Grand American Avenue 1850–1920 Exhibit the two students who were working there helped install objects and artifacts that had been culled from across the country to best represent the finest American boulevards. Among these objects was an ornate lamppost top that had once hung along part of Wilshire Boulevard in Los Angeles. Even though they had to provide the muscle to move the wrought iron ornamental top, the students told me with a great deal of satisfaction and pride in their eyes, that they had indeed *installed* this object. They had clearly bonded with the artifact, and, in doing so, made a personal connection to the past. These two students worked at the Octagon during it's multiyear restoration. They worked on all aspects of the project from cleaning the interior of the roof with special vacuums to assisting the chief preservationist with documentation about the restoration. The entire experience was so rewarding that one of the young men decided to pursue art history in college.

Other students who have worked with Birk have helped her with the extensive archival photograph collection the museum holds of architect Richard Morris Hunt's Biltmore House, designed for George Washington Vanderbilt and located in Ashville, North Carolina. These images, all taken in the 1890s, had to be encapsulated in special, acid-free holders. Again on one of my visits, I watched as the two students carefully moved the pictures into their new protective sleeves. While on the surface this may sound rather innocuous, I assure you that it was not. Birk is always quick to explain to her interns the why of what they are doing. Records of any sort are important markers of the past, and in the case of Biltmore House, these photographs document from start to finish the labor that went into building the largest single-family home in the United States. By working to preserve the memory of the past, the students learn not only the technical skills needed to keep collective memory alive, but also to understand the philosophical basis for such action.

One bonus for students working at the Octagon is that Birk treats them like fellow staff members. Whenever there is an exhibit opening during the tenure of the interns, they are always invited to participate, and they almost always do.

A number of students each year like to work with Mike Henry at Colvin Run Mill. Colvin Run Mill is a nineteenth-century grist mill located in Great Falls, Virginia. As part of the public programming of the mill, an active nineteenth-century blacksmith forge is operated at the site. Henry, a historian and trained blacksmith interpreter, takes the novice interns and molds them into apprentice blacksmiths. They spend many hours sweating over the forge at the mill, learning the trade as it was done over one hundred years ago. Often their faces are black with grime as they pound out with a hammer on an anvil whatever object Henry has directed them to create. During the course of their internship, they make by hand a number of objects that can be purchased by the public—objects such as S-hooks or fireplace pokers. In addition, by the end of the internship, they have to be able to explain to the public exactly what they are doing, how they are doing it, and why they are doing it. Each year, Henry arranges for the students to participate in a living history program whereby his forge is used at a Civil War reenactment to create authentic-looking materials for the reenactors. Frequently at these reenactments, the neophyte blacksmiths have camped out with the reenactors, becoming part of the encampment. Often they use the materials they have made to help cook their food over a campfire. When I make my inspection visit, the young blacksmiths always show me what they have made and tell me in detail how they made it. Generally I am also told just how their hard work is. My reply, "It's good for your soul."

Participating in an activity of a more Colonial American vintage are the young ladies who work at either the Carlyle House, a 1752 property in Old Town Alexandria, Virginia, or at Gunston Hall, the 1754 home of Virginia patriot George Mason. At both sites, interns work not only with the curators responsible for collections management, but also as interpreters of the houses during their respective open-house programs. Carlyle House's claim to fame is that it was in the parlor of John Carlyle's residence that General Edward Braddock of the British Army first proposed that the colonies should be taxed to pay for their own defenses against the French and Indians. Each year in the spring, Carlyle House sponsors Braddock Day, a kind of living history festival where costumed interpreters, including my students, guide people through the grounds and house. One year I had two interns who were part of a Northern Virginia living history organization. They were extensively involved in first-person interpretation of the home. When I visited them they refused to break character even to talk to me, their teacher!

Later, I was informed by them, tongue in cheek, that they very much enjoyed not having to address me in twentieth-century fashion. I must say I was very impressed with the knowledge that they could convey about the house during their skits.

On Kite Day held each March at Gunston Hall, my student interns, also dressed up in period costume, work in the children's tent, leading youngsters in all manner of Colonial games. Here they do third-person interpretation, not only in the children's tent but also in the Colonial kitchen, demonstrating for the public how the kitchen at George Mason's home would have been operated.

In the case of both Carlyle House and Gunston Hall the students not only have to use superior people skills, but they also have to have mastery of the history of the site in order to be able to help tell the story of the property. True, they could learn the history of the site by reading books, but at both sites students learn by doing, having been trained in a much different fashion than a standard textbook. Sometimes these students read a number of primary source materials related to the property in order to get a better sense of the place.

In Chapter 1 I briefly discussed my students and their working with Mike Johnson, one of the chief archeologists in Fairfax County. The thing I really like about Johnson is how much passion he brings to his work and how that passion rubs off on the student interns who work for him. Johnson provides these students with not only the big picture of archeology in Fairfax County, but also with the necessary details that make up that big picture. Mike's area of expertise is prehistoric archeology, that is archeology prior to 1600, though as was the case with the Civil War soldiers, he can quickly adjust to historic archeology. Most of the archeology that Johnson and my student interns work with is American Indian archeology. Whether it's in the lab—where the students work to sort rock fragments by category—or out in the field—where they are ever so gently digging up the soil—Johnson is there to ensure that they get the most out of their experience.

These students are not just used for manual labor, but actually become amateur archeologists by virtue of what they accomplish. Whenever a significant find is discovered in either the lab or out in the field, Johnson halts work and brings together the students so that he can discuss with them what they have uncovered, perhaps an Indian projectile point or a piece of Indian pottery. Very rarely do the students have to interact with the public, rather they often have to bring together and use the skills that they have acquired in the other classes they have taken at West Springfield, particularly math and science. Students have to have an understanding of mathematical problem solving when they work out in the field. Quite often one will hear all kinds of scientific terms bandied about, like stratigraphy, when a dig is ongoing. Many times exact measurements have to be taken and recorded as material is brought forth or discovered in the soil, as the story of the place being worked on comes to the forefront. Students who work with Johnson are also trained to use the host of tools needed by archeologists, tools ranging from shovels and trowels to compasses and fluid measurers.

These students labor very intently, but always come back filled with stories about their particular adventures. By the look in their eyes, you can tell that for some it has been a life-transforming experience.

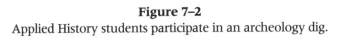

Figure 7–2
Applied History students participate in an archeology dig.

Internship possibilities have been and continue to be limitless. Many students have worked with original primary source documents, some have given excellent tours of places such as the Woodrow Wilson Home, while others who are caught up in the technology craze have created websites for their internships. Further adventures and opportunities are still down the road. I encourage you to snoop around your environment and tap into your local community resources. See what's out there for you and your students to become involved with as volunteers or as interns. Even if you're not in a position to create a course of this nature consider sponsoring a student to work at a local historical society or museum property. You will be glad that you did.

Eight

On the Road Again
Field Trips

Well, this is the end of a perfect day, near the end of a journey, too.
Carrie Jacobs Bond

I leaned back into the big comfortable chair of the charter bus and closed my eyes. Filling my ears was a cacophony of voices. All of us including the students and the parent chaperones were ready for the long ride home. I said to myself, "Did I really pull this one off? Come on Jim, you've got to be in a dream world. How in the world did I manage to lure twenty-some students and close to a dozen parents down to a remote corner of southwestern Georgia, 700 plus miles away from home and on a weekend to boot?" Then I realized that my thoughts were the same ones that permeated my brain after I had taken students on a visit to Frank Lloyd Wright's Falling Water, the marvelous home he designed over a waterfall for a wealthy Pittsburgh family, in Bear Run, Pennsylvania; or the trip we took to walk across the Brooklyn Bridge; or the visit to the Fort McHenry parade ground that withstood the 1814 bombardment from the British fleet, where we folded a replica of the flag—the original Star Spangled Banner—that flew over Fort McHenry in Baltimore, Maryland; or the excursion to Thomas Jefferson's Monticello, nestled on the top of a hill that overlooks Charlottesville, Virginia.

Field trips: There simply isn't a better way to teach and learn history. On a field trip, you can get out and walk around where "the stuff of the past has happened." And the best part is doing it with your students. A kind of energy happens between you and your students when you encounter history in this dynamic fashion: The place you are visiting becomes, in its entirety, a teachable moment that will be long remembered by you and your students. Not only have you given your time to your students, you have also opened a window to a much deeper kind of learning, the kind that lasts for a lifetime. If I had my way, I'd load all of my students on a bus and travel around the countryside, much as Doug Brinkley did with one of his college courses, so wonderfully described in his book, *The Majic Bus.*

Using field trips effectively can help you surpass your instructional goals, because they allow students to stand in the footprints of history. Historical reality becomes palpable when you visit a place where history happened.

Often students tell me that their field experience was "fun." At some level that is probably true, but I would prefer it if they used the word "enjoyable." To have enjoyed the experience captures the dynamic and total-learning experience that takes place when visiting a historic site, be it a battlefield or historic house museum or property. Visiting a site serves as a bridge to understanding the past perhaps more than any tool available in the immediate classroom.

Starting Off on the Right Foot

I have alluded to field trips in previous chapters, but here I would like to discuss the how's and why's of putting together a successful field trip. The three trips explored in this chapter are all part of a larger whole and are attached to units of study. It is my intent that you recognize that what I have put together in the other chapters of this book comes to fruition on these field trips.

Your field trip is more likely to succeed if you follow these guidelines.

Do Your Homework

As with any activity you prepare for your classes, you must do your homework prior to any visit. Your homework not only entails the necessary historical background reading about your chosen visit site, but also the actual planning of the trip—from arranging transportation to securing lodging and meals if needed. If possible, visit the site yourself before the field trip. Your preview will enhance your familiarity with the site, including any special programs—such as slide shows or living history presentations—the museum or historic site offers. Many historic sites and museums have extensive education outreach programs. If you call ahead, you can find out what kinds of materials the site or museum have created to help you in getting the maximum out of your visit. Sometimes the educational curators have prepared previsit materials that you can use with your students to prepare them for the trip. Sites also may have specific hands-on activities in which students can participate once they are on site, but do be certain that they are age appropriate. If you think a docent or guide may "talk down" to your students, politely explain that this won't be necessary; the guide will probably be relieved to deliver his or her message at an adult level.

Some trips require more extensive work than other trips. Overnight trips can sometimes take months of planning that, if done right, can reap big rewards. Be sure to follow your school district's regulations regarding field trips. Don't forget to recruit and involve the parents of the students. Many times parents gain just as much from the trip as their sons or daughters. Having parents participate in a successful field trip can also bolster your program for the future. Parents can drive on local trips if you put together a caravan journey. Without a doubt, parents are important allies.

Conduct Previsit and Postvisit Activities

Conduct previsit learning activities as well as postvisit activities in order to ensure that students get the best kind of experience from their visit—an experience where their intellect and their emotional intelligence blend into a kind of holistic understanding. Once again, be certain your visit fits in context with what you and your classes are studying. Field trips should support the main goals of your instruction and work as an enrichment activity. Sometimes an exception to this rule may be appropriate, if a particular event, traveling exhibit, or theater performance does not occur when the topic is being studied in class. Many times the historic site or museum have put together exceptional materials that I have used; while other times, as in the cases discussed in this chapter, I have created my own material or merged it with the site's material. For closure, I like to use journal entries or assign research essays tied to the visit. Sometimes I use a combination of both in my assessment. In any case, it is imperative that you hold a debriefing session with your students shortly after the trip in order to determine not only what they learned, but also how you might better prepare students for future visits. Students will be honest with you and at times it makes good sense to consider their suggestions.

I think one of the reasons that I've had such success with field trips is that I have listened to my students and accepted their criticisms with an eye toward future trips. Quite often, when I have heeded a previous class' advice, the second time around the experience is much better for everyone.

Take Your Camera

Finally, take your camera along and suggest the same for your students and their parents. Documenting these trips in photographs can help you as a teacher, particularly if you take slides and show them to your class a week or so after the experience to put closure on the trip. Or you can create a photo essay of the trip, laminate it, and display it in your classroom. Either way it again shows your students that you have a vested interest in them and their learning. For students and their parents, the photographs can provide a window to the past that they can look into years after the students have left high school. I like to tell everyone it all becomes a part of their personal history.

I have discovered that one of the most rewarding aspects of taking my Applied History classes on field trips is that they help build bonds and community within the class. I enjoy watching friendships emerge between students who before their Applied History experience hardly knew each other. Leading field trips also puts me in better touch with my students. I can engage them in conversations about themselves in an effort to get to know them better. Although we may talk about our final destination and its academic relevance, it's more important for me, in these situations, to talk with my students about where they are planning to apply to college, how their social life is going, what they are doing in school, and what's going on with their life in general. Informal conversations like these help me understand my students and thus teach them more effectively.

Finally I want my students to have what I call the *Sistine Chapel Experience*. This personal experience of mine, perhaps more than any other, fostered my belief in learning and its connection to the concept of understanding. When I was sixteen, I went to Italy. As part of our tour of the Vatican, we were brought to the Sistine Chapel.

Being raised Catholic and attending a church that at that time used high art to help fulfill its mission, I had long been a fan of Michelangelo. Before this trip I read Irving Stone's *The Agony and the Ecstasy.* I had also seen the motion picture of the same name, and always marveled at how Michelangelo had laid on his back for four years as he painted that enormous fresco. I loved to look at books that were richly illustrated with art that he created. I can remember the many times that I studied in our school library a book that had a color foldout of the entire ceiling of the Sistine Chapel. When I first stepped into the chamber of the Sistine Chapel, a transformation overtook me. Despite all of the times I had looked at the pictures and read about this magnificent work of art, I really didn't understand it until I saw it with my own eyes. Only then could I feel the true emotion that emanates from Michelangelo's brush strokes. Seeing it in person made all the difference in the world. This is what I want to happen to my students when we go on field trips. I don't expect them to replicate my feelings, for that is something personal and unique to all of us at such moments. Rather, I want them in their own way to come away from these experiences with a kind of "Ah ha! Now I know!" sentiment, fully making the leap and bridging the intellect with the affect. Doing so makes the learning circle and process complete.

Gettysburg

The one site I have visited most often—with and without my students—is Gettysburg National Military Park in Gettysburg, Pennsylvania. The first time I visited Gettysburg, I was ten; I've lost count how many times since then that I've returned. My students and I have walked the battleground in sunshine, rain, and when it's been covered in an ethereal mist. Every time it's been a good experience.

When I first took my students to Gettysburg I would hire a Gettysburg Licensed Battlefield Guide to lead us on the tour; but as I became more familiar with the battle and began my own investigation, I decided that I could give a tour more tailored to what I wanted the students to learn from the visit. So now I lead the contingent of students every year, armed with material that I have created and developed. But before we visit, I prepare my students thoroughly for the experience.

Preparing for the Visit

For starters, I show students slides of the battlefield that I have taken over the last fifteen years. In addition to showing the landscape, I include archival images of key figures who played a role in the battle, including Robert E. Lee, George Meade, and Joshua Lawrence Chamberlain, as well as the noted period photographs taken by Alexander Gardner's and Matthew Brady's studios during the days immediately following the battle. I also include slides of images that I have taken from Don Troiani and Brian Pohanka's book, *Don Troiani's Civil War*. I explain to students that no action photographs exist of the battle, as photography was in its infancy; and the artist who has best captured the fighting is, in fact, Troiani. A contemporary commercial artist, Troiani has produced a whole series, based on exhaustive research, on the Battle of Gettysburg, and the images fit nicely into the history as I interpret it for the students. The students also read *The Killer Angels* by Michael Shaara as well as some primary source material from battle participants. In addition we watch *Gettysburg*, which is based on Shaara's novel.

As part of class preparation for the visit, I also conduct a class on the history of the photography of the battle. For my resource I rely on William

Frassanito's landmark work, *Gettysburg: A Journey in Time*. Through extensive research Frassanito has proved that some of the photographs taken at Gettysburg were staged for the camera, including one of the most famous images from the battle—that of a dead Confederate soldier in Devils Den. Frassanito believes that this dead soldier was found near the site, but that his body was moved to create a more compelling image. Making overhead transparencies from the photographs and diagrams in Frassanito's book, I lead the students in an examination of this possibility because this location will be one of the stops on our visit.

During the class period before the visit takes place, I provide students with an image that I discovered several years ago when I was reading Richard Moe's *The Last Full Measure: The Life and Death of the First Minnesota Volunteers*. It is a wartime photograph of two brothers, Patrick Henry Taylor and Isaac Lyman Taylor, both of whom saw action at Gettysburg. I ask students to study the photographs and consider the faces of the two men. Then I explain that we will talk about these two men during the tour—as I put it, we will meet them during our visit.

During the Visit

When our caravan arrives at Gettysburg, I first give students about a half-hour to visit the National Park Service Visitor Center and museum. Then it's out onto the battlefield. About four years ago, I began to pull together some battle accounts in the words of the participants. I have collected them in a three-ring binder, and as we stop at various locations, I read about what happened at that location through the words of those who witnessed the carnage. Our tour stops include the Lutheran Seminary, the site where on the first day Union First Corps Commander, John Reynolds, was killed; we proceed along the Confederate battle line to one of the two Park Service towers, which we climb, that give a panoramic view of the battlefield, over to the Devils Den. Here we study the location where photographers Gardner and Timothy O'Sullivan allegedly posed the dead Confederate soldier. I observe the expressions of the students as they come face-to-face with a historical reality, that, until this point, even though they had only seen it in a photograph, has been an abstraction. Suddenly I can see flashing through their minds, "Ah ha. So this is what we were looking at. Now I understand it." From this vantage point, students can also see for themselves the slope that the Confederate soldiers surged up on the second day of fighting. Each year, students marvel at the notion that anyone would have tried to take that hill under the kind of fire that was pouring down on them. And each year, a contingent of students decides to walk or run to the top of Little Round Top. Catching up with those who have assaulted the hill, the rest of us then walk the crest of the precarious Union defenses on Little Round Top, including back into the woods where the 20th Maine made their heroic stand. Again, as we make each stop, I recite a selected reading.

Just before we break for lunch, we come to the First Minnesota Monument along the extended Union lines that run across Cemetery Ridge. On July 2, 1863, this was the scene of some very intense combat activity. Into the vortex of battle the First Minnesota was sent to plug a hole in the Union line. When they began their charge, two hundred sixty-two men assaulted the rushing Confederates. When the First Minnesota had done its duty only forty-seven men were standing: a casualty rate of 82 percent. I have the students sit on the base of the monument and I pass out photographs of the Taylor brothers. I ask them to look at the images. Finally, I read from Moe's book the moving journal entry of Henry Taylor, in which Taylor describes having found his dead brother's body on the battlefield as well as excerpts from the letters that Taylor sent back to his parents and sister informing them of their son's and their brother's death.

> About 8:30, Mr. Snow of Company B tells me he thinks he saw my brother, and I accompany him to the spot, and I find my dear brother dead! A shell struck him on the top of his head and passed out through his back, cutting his belt in two. The poor fellow did not know what hit him. I secured his pocketbook, watch, diary, knife, etc., and with Wm. E. Cundy and J.S. Brown buried him at 10 o'clock A.M., 350 paces west of a road which passes north and south by the house of Jacob Hummelbaugh and John Swisher (colored) and equi-distant from each, and by a stone wall where he fell, about a mile south of Gettysburg. I placed a board at his head on which I inscribed:

> No useless coffin enclosed his breast,
> Nor in sheet nor shroud we bound him,
> But he lay like a warrior taking his rest,
> With his shelter tent around him.

Part of the letter that Henry Taylor wrote to his parents informing them of Isaac's death reads:

> Isaac has not fallen in vain. What though one of your six soldiers has fallen on the altar of our country. 'Tis a glorious death; better die free than live slaves . . . He wrote in his diary while on the field of battle before killed. I cannot express to you my sorrow at his loss. I feel as though I was all alone.

> Your and my country's
> Henry

To his sister Taylor wrote:

Figure 8–1
Patrick Henry Taylor *(l)* and Isaac Lyman Taylor *(r)*.

Isaac was a brave soldier, and his calmness and coolness in action had
been spoken of frequently by many of his comrades. I have always been
proud of his conduct in battle . . . July third, half past eight, a man of
Company G (Snow) was coming up with some coffee for some of the
officers, and saw Isaac lying dead—he told me he thought he saw my
brother—killed. I went with him to the spot and found it to be too true,
secured his things—knapsack, haversack, and canteen were gone. He
probably threw them off when he went into action. I found a spade and
took William E. Cundy and James L. Brown of Company E and went
and dug his grave. We laid him down with all his clothes on, as he fell,
and spread a shelter tent over him. As we laid him down, I remarked,
Well Isaac, all I can give you is a soldiers grave. I then sat down on a
stone while the two comrades buried him. I was the only one to weep
over his grave—his Father, Mother, brothers, and sisters were all ignorant of his death . . .

These readings place in graphic perspective just one of the total of 51,000
casualties who fell over those three days in July. We break for lunch in
silence.

After lunch, we cross back over to the place along the Confederate
battle line, Seminary Ridge, from where Lee watched the famous Pickett's
Charge unfold. I make sure that students recall the scene in the film *Gettysburg* where close to 15,000 men move out and across the open ground
into immortality. Asking them to let their minds' eyes wander, I again
read to students the words of the men who crossed that field on July 3,
1863. I ask them to imagine the sounds of the bugles and see the hundreds of battle standards unfurled in the hot July sun. Then we take off to
recreate their march, walking the one mile distance to the center of the
Union line crossing the terrain that is not much different than it was in
1863. As they walk, the students begin to realize that the terrain is
uneven as they trudge across the battlefield. Once we reach the Union
line, we stop and again I read to them accounts of what the furious frenzy
of battle was like as the Confederates almost succeeded in penetrating the
Union defenses. When the day is over, we are all physically and emotion-
ally drained; usually the ninety-minute ride back to Springfield, Virginia
is quiet.

Journal Entries

Before I assign students their journal entries on the visit, I give them some
time to reflect on what they have experienced, so rather then do a journal assignment on the battlefield—which I have considered doing—I wait
until the next time we meet at school as a class, and before we debrief, I
have them respond in their journals. Here is what some of the students
have said: "I thoroughly enjoyed our trip to Gettysburg, Pennsylvania. It

Figure 8–2

Class at Gettysburg, seated on the base of the *Virginia Monument* before retracing Pickett's Charge.

was amazing to see and walk the distance that the men in the battle had to go to fight. When we walked Pickett's Charge I was surprised that anyone could survive walking across that field with all the cannon and gunfire around them. When I turned around, the view was fabulous. I couldn't believe that I had that distance that men had fought and died on. Nothing could have the same effect on me, not reading a book, or even watching a film about the battle. The 'hands-on' experience of Gettysburg was truly an unforgettable trip and I am so glad to have gone." Another student wrote, "I've never been to Gettysburg and I thought it was a good experience. It brought me closer to the battle and being in the actual place where it happened was very meaningful, especially when we went up the hill (Little Round Top). Running up the hill was tiring and the thought of carrying guns, fighting and things like that would be even worse. I just can't imagine how anyone could go through with that and survive. My Dad [a chaperone] brought up the fact when we were on the top of Little Round Top looking down that after the battle there were hundreds of dead bodies on that hill. It was very spiritual and unimaginable, I could barely take it in."

The Bedford, Virginia D-Day Veterans

On a good day you can see the Peaks of Otter for miles around. They stand out against the horizon as part of the scenery that make up the Blue Ridge Mountains. As you enter the town, some two hundred or so miles southwest of Washington, D.C., you are greeted by a sign that reads, "Bedford, Virginia: The World's Best Small Town." Until June 6, 1944, Bedford's single claim to fame was that it was the home of the International Elks Club. But on that fateful day in world history, Bedford found itself forever changed by events that took place a whole ocean away. If sacrifices during war are measured by the grief a community feels, then Bedford stands out as no other community in the American annals of World War II. In the first fifteen minutes in the gray dawn of the Normandy coast at a beach—code-named Omaha—nineteen of Bedford's sons, brothers, and fathers perished in the opening wave of the assault on Hitler's Atlantic Wall during Operation Overlord. By the end of the day, two more men from Bedford would pay the ultimate price and this small town would find its place on the map distinguished because of the number of its men lost in the opening moment to drive oppression and tyranny from Europe. They were part of the largest armed force ever engineered for a single military objective in the history of the world, and they knew that they were taking part in a drama that would be the defining moment, albeit at an early age, of their lives. The small farming town whose 1944 population totaled 3,200 was the home of Company A, a National Guard unit federalized in 1941 on the eve of American participation in the war. Out of the 190-man company that went ashore on Omaha Beach, ninety-one men lost their lives, sixty-four sustained wounds, and only fifteen were able to continue in combat.

On June 16 word of what had happened to "the Best of Bedford"—men who had never witnessed combat before—began to come in over the Western Union Telegraph wires, located in Green's Drugstore, a typical corner business that for many, in the rural farm community, was a place of social gathering. All the messages began in the same way, "The Secretary of War regrets to inform you . . ." It would be a year before anyone had the nerve to gather there in large groups again.

I first heard of Bedford in 1994 during the Fiftieth Anniversary of the D-Day landings. The story of what happened to this community was both compelling and captivating. Bedford and its veterans, those men from Company A of the 29th Infantry Division, 116th Regiment, received much attention during the Diamond Anniversary. The survivors were interviewed and major newspapers such as *USA Today* and *The Washington Post* ran cover stories; National Public Radio did a feature broadcast live from downtown Bedford. Soon thereafter I found myself poking around to find out as much as I could about Bedford and its role in D-Day.

As I continued to conduct my research for my classes, I put together a packet of oral histories consisting of material given by some of the veterans I was able to locate in a number of D-Day oral histories that were published around the time of the Fiftieth Anniversary. Initially I created a Historical Head for my U.S. History class, but I really wanted to do much more for my Applied History students.

In the meantime, the Bedford veterans, and other interested parties, were moving along with plans to build the National D-Day Memorial in Bedford. I arranged through my contacts there to have my students meet with some of the surviving veterans of Company A.

Planning the Trip

Planning was essential. A week before our visit, I provided students with the oral history packet I had collected. I asked them to read it before our visit because they would be meeting with some of the men whose accounts they were reading. I also gave them literature sent to me by the National D-Day Memorial Foundation that explained the memorial project. Finally, I showed the class Charles Guggenheim's film *D-Day* from *The American Experience* series.

Meeting the Veterans of Company A

On a gray, October day, not unlike June 6, 1944, we arrived at the restaurant where we were to meet the veterans and have lunch. The restaurant was located in the former train station, where these men had shipped off to war. We were warmly greeted by Pride Wingfield and several men, all over the age of seventy, including Roy Stevens, Ray Nance, and Bob Sales. Linda Kochendarfer, communications manager for the Memorial Foundation, was also there. A conference room at the restaurant had been set aside specifically for this meeting and added an atmosphere of intimacy to our meeting. Shortly after lunch, Linda greeted all of us on behalf of the town of Bedford, and as she was a member of the Bedford City Council, presented each of us with a token of their appreciation of our visit. I watched with admiration as the veterans handed each student a lapel pin and then watched every student affix them to their clothing. It was a kind of gift from one generation to another. One of my colleagues, who was assisting on the trip, videotaped the interaction. As the students and veterans conversed, I stayed on the sidelines.

The students posed some of the following questions:

- What were your thoughts moments before the invasion?
- Were you aware of the enormity of this event?
- Did your particular boat get to shore?

Figure 8–3

E. Ray Nance, Co. A veteran, talks about the landing at Omaha Beach.

- Were you scared when you got into the landing craft?
- What is combat really like?
- Did it seem real? Was it like a dream? How would you describe it?

The veterans answered each of these questions; but mostly it was their individual stories that captivated everyone in the room. Ray Nance, a Lieutenant on D-Day, said that landing on the beach was like "going up the red dragon's throat," and that there are no human words possible to describe what they saw, that it was beyond imagination.

Roy Stevens, who lost his twin brother Ray, related how his brother had extended him his hand as they prepared to hit the beach, but that he told his brother he would shake it on land when they were in the beach exit draw—the routes off the beach. Roy expressed his regret in not shaking his brother's hand because they never met in the exit draw.

Bob Sales told the students that of the thirty-three men in his landing craft, he was the only one who survived. His voice cracked with emotion as he described his sprint to the sea wall some two-and-a-half football fields inland. When he reached the wall, he turned around looking for his companions only to find he was the only one who made it. Sales also told the students that the landing parties were

Figure 8–4
Students at the *Omaha Beach Memorial.*

under such heavy small arms and artillery fire that if "you moved on you were in trouble on Omaha Beach."

All of the men talked about the dead bodies bumping around the water and that sometimes they recognized the faces of the fallen. They talked with familiarity about the men who never returned, men whom they had known for a long time, friends who had grown up together. I could tell that my students had never encountered history in quite this fashion before, and I believe that their lives were all the richer for it.

After our luncheon, we split up into two groups. One half of the students went and visited the Bedford City/County Museum while the other half went over to the National D-Day Memorial Foundation office. Each group also took time to pause and examine the simple Bedford D-Day Memorial erected by the community and placed in front of the court-house. The names of the men from Bedford who perished on D-Day are on a bronze plaque affixed to a shaft of stone that came from Omaha Beach. After each group was done at their particular location, we switched.

Ellen Wandrei, curator and manager of the museum, gave the students a tour of the museum. The Bedford City/County Museum is a small museum run with a very few staff members. Part of my reasoning for bringing my class down to Bedford was to see the value of local history exhibits. I wanted the students to realize that the D-Day story from Bedford means a great deal to the local community. I think many of the students were sensitized by their visit.

Across the way at the National D-Day Memorial Foundation office, Linda Kochendarfer shared with the students the ambitious plans for the National D-Day Memorial. We happened to be visiting Bedford in the wake of some very good news. The previous day, *Peanuts* cartoonist Charles Shultz, a World War II veteran, had donated one million dollars to the building fund for the memorial. By having a field trip at this moment in time the students were able to see just what goes into the creation of memorials of this scope.

Our last two stops included a visit to the Bedford Cemetery, where some of the men who perished on D-Day were buried, and the site for the memorial. Our visit to the cemetery particularly stands out. Out of the twenty-one who lost their lives, several men were brought home, some were left in the National Cemetery that overlooks Omaha Beach, while in a few cases no bodies were recovered. The Company A men, including their captain, Taylor Fellers, are buried near each other. Some of the men have simple grave markers flush to the ground, bearing their name, rank, and date of birth followed by the date June 6, 1944. As we stood in the rain at the cemetery, I wondered what was going on in the minds of my students.

After the Visit

During our debriefing, the students clearly indicated that the trip was a wonderful learning opportunity. They were very animated in discussion. The consensus that I got in talking with my students was that they felt very special in having met these veterans. It was obvious that the stories told by the veterans had moved them. Their journal writings also expressed this sentiment. One student wrote:

> This was such a memorable experience! Nothing could come closer to really understanding what these men went through than actually speaking with them. And I was so privileged to have been able to do this since I know we are probably the last generation to be able to speak with war veterans who fought that type of war—a war where you saw the enemy right in front of you. But even on hearing their tragic stories, though vividly told, I still cannot imagine what they had to go through . . . it was really overpowering!

Thinking back over the experience I reflected on the words spoken by Rod Steiger's character in the film *The Longest Day*, "You remember it. Remember every bit of it. Cause we are on the eve of a day that people are going to talk about long after you and I are dead and gone. You want to know something, it gives me goose pimples just to be part of it."

Andersonville

The clay surface of the ground is bright reddish-orange, a hue defined naturally by the laws of chemistry reflecting its deep iron content as well as symbolically by the valor and anguish of those who endured this place more than one hundred years ago. That's the thing that resonates within me every time I come to Andersonville. Now I know why they used to make bricks from this clay; it is so hard to walk on that there is virtually no give to it. So I can't even begin to imagine what it must have been like to sleep on it. But for those Union prisoners of war who spent a living hell just existing in this place that was almost all they had for a bed.

The class trip to Andersonville National Historic Site is the culminating activity for our term research unit on the prison itself and the subsequent imprisonment and trial of Henry Wirz.

As the charter bus we were in pulled up to and through the site entrance, I pointed out to my students the National Cemetery. No longer did the men who suffered and died at Andersonville remain frozen figures in a vacuum for my students. Even the period photographic images, taken of the men before they were captured, that we had looked at earlier in the year as we began the project suddenly had a new immediacy about them.

The students had already written an exhaustive research paper, spending time poring over vintage primary source documents at the National Archives, drawing conclusions, and weighing evidence. They had examined countless images, photographed in 1864, of the camp, read the accounts of numerous prisoners, read poetry composed by both prisoners and people who had ancestors perish there, and studied other material related to the site. Even as a class we watched the Turner Film production of *Andersonville*. But all of that did not coalesce until we walked through the site of the camp and the cemetery.

I believe that if students are to understand history, they have to bring together intellect and emotional intelligence. I know that there is no possible way to really *know* what the past was like, but I believe that we can get close, particularly with visits to the place where history really happened. That's why I wanted to bring my class to Andersonville.

It was marvelous to watch the students take so well to the site. I could sense the power that the place had over them, not only because they were on historic ground, but because as a result of their intense study they now had a vested interest in Andersonville. They had a certain familiarity with the site.

We looked over the area that had been the sinks—the latrine, so to speak—that was constructed along the stockades only water supply, Stockade Branch, where the diseases that killed most of the prisoners were incubated. I asked the students to imagine that place on a hot, humid summer day in 1864 and see the interior of the prison pen and smell the air that permeated the ground. I asked them to imagine being crammed together so that each of them had only six square feet to themselves, just like the prisoners did.

When we walked through the replica of the North Gate, I hustled them into its center and closed the door behind them. Inside, they were sealed off from the world outside and the prison pen on the other side, in a kind of limbo. Again, I asked them to imagine what it must have been like to have escaped the carnage of the battlefield only to find themselves by a cruel twist of fate facing a different sort of hell.

That evening we were transported back in time, to 1864, at the height of the camp's population, some 33,000 plus men were then packed into the twenty-six acre compound. The ghosts from the past who transported us back along the continuum of time were reenactors and Park Service staff who played the roles of both prisoner and guard. We were led by a single individual, a concerned citizen of the period, holding a lantern, to the stockade perimeter where several guards and their sergeant permitted us to pass into the compound. The guards did not appear to be enjoying their jobs and the sense of their suffering and endurance was felt by all. Once inside the stockade we encountered the sick, the dying, and the disgruntled—men of the Union Army who felt that they were just wasting away while the war dragged on without them. A preacher, played by Alan Marsh, took us to the side of a dying man and we stood transfixed as the preacher offered a prayer for the redemption of his soul. Before long it was time to return to the twentieth century and the same lone specter who had led us back in time took us back into the present.

As we returned to our bus I could hear groups of students and parent chaperones talking about how powerful an experience they had just had. The words "awesome" and "cool" were bandied about freely by the students.

Early the next day we returned to the cemetery where we were given a first-rate tour by Park Ranger, Alan Marsh. As we started at one end of the twenty-acre cemetery and walked across the graves of the men, which were only three feet below the surface, Marsh periodically would choose one of the students and have the student read from a prisoner's diary or journal. The one feature that stands out so clearly in the cemetery is that the graves are numbered in the same sequence as the men who died were buried. The first graves are several paces apart, but there is a different kind of chronology told as you move among the headstones. It's not hard to notice the impact of the soaring death rate because as the

Figure 8–5
The National Cemetery at Andersonville National Historic Site.

death toll climbed, the headstones got closer and closer together until they almost touched one another. The largest section of the cemetery is nothing but a sea of stone. Alan finished his tour at the most appropriate place possible, the Illinois State Monument, which is a statue of History standing over two children and holding them close to her side, pointing out at the endless rows of headstones, beckoning them to learn from the past. Marsh's concluding remarks were, "that we must take in History's viewpoint and never forget what happened here at Andersonville."

On the way home I asked not only that the students provide me with some written evaluation of the trip, but I also asked the parent chaperones to respond. One of the benefits of conducting this sort of exercise, a field trip of this scope and nature, is that it's also a pleasure to include the adults in the learning experience.

One father recorded:

> History is not black and white. Reading history and learning from textbooks and lectures in a classroom environment can fuel one's imagination. But it is not until one experiences and senses what has transpired that true learning occurs. Therein lies the enormous value of experiences such as the Andersonville field trip.

Another parent wrote:

John Donne once wrote that each death diminishes us all. Certainly when that death occurs before its time, it is impossible to determine the loss. The more than 12,000 that died at Andersonville, however, serve to remind us of the pain we all inflict on one another for the sake of a cause and the pain we can endure for the sake of another . . . Andersonville reminds us that POWs were/are people, people who suffer not just a loss of freedom but a loss of dignity and human rights. As we approach the 21st century, words and phrases such as genocide and ethnic cleansing are still heard on the 6:00 news. The experiences of the past have not been sufficient to teach us that we must treat with compassion those who fall into our hands during times of war. Perhaps the students, having heard and seen the history of Andersonville, will want to influence policies and politics of the future so that places like Andersonville can only be found in the past.

Summing up the experiences of the students, one wrote:

There are times when words cannot explain the emotions that are evoked upon seeing a place like Andersonville. To hear about and research it was one thing, but to sit upon the soil and touch the ground upon which numerous men suffered and died is quite another thing in itself. I sat on the soil, with my hands on the ground, and it was as if I was soaking up the pain. No book can replicate that for me.

And for me as a teacher no experience can replicate the learning and teaching that a thoughtful and well-planned field trip can afford to everyone who participates. So as the bus pulled into the driveway of West Springfield High School after the twelve-hour ride home, I found myself musing about other pathways to the past I would be traveling with my students. Whatever it is and wherever we go, it is sure to be another adventure.

Some Final Thoughts

Remember that historical events and the lives of people who went before us took place in all regions of the country. No area is void of a historical past and memory. Give serious consideration to taking your students to local museums and the places around you where the "stuff" of history happened. In time you may develop a more adventurous soul and be willing to take your students far afield to explore and learn about the past.

Epilogue

Far and away the best prize that life offers is the opportunity to
work hard at work worth doing.

                                                    Theodore Roosevelt

A "teacher," Henry Adams declared in his *Education of Henry Adams*, "affects eternity; he can never tell where his influence stops." Most teachers recognize and appreciate this maxim with an understanding that by and large they will not know how far and wide their influence will go. This is all part of what I call the mystery of teaching. Teaching is something that can't be defined or quantified. What makes me a good teacher is not the same thing that makes you a good teacher. Each of us needs to discover for ourselves our own particular "mystery." To this day I can't exactly tell you what makes me a success in the classroom; it's probably not one thing but a whole combination of factors.

In this book I've tried to outline for you some ideas that have been wonderfully successful in my classroom. Some of the ideas I've developed are unique to me while others are a combination of ideas that I have drawn from a whole host of individuals. Try them as I have outlined them, or better yet, put your own twist to them. Remember, first and above all, be yourself. I think that this element is at the very heart of good teaching. With the wave of technology we are experiencing there are all kinds of new things to be tried in the classroom. Before you commit yourself to using a new CD-ROM or program off the Internet, preview it and be sure that you are comfortable with the material. However, never forget the value and power of the written word and its place in the study of history. Be certain to instill that idea in your students.

Keep in mind that teaching is also about building relationships. In our particular case it's about building relationships between the past and the present, as well as creating and nurturing relationships with our students and colleagues.

I feel very fortunate to be a history teacher at this precise moment in our national history. Despite what the press or the pundits might lead you to believe there is a great deal of "good news" in the arena of history teaching. Today we embrace a heritage education that is inclusive of all the peoples, races, creeds, religions, and cultures who have helped to build this nation. Teachers and scholars are willing to deal with sensitive issues that have helped and continue to help define our national identity, particularly issues regarding race relations. It's important that our students wrestle with those things about America that are not necessarily positive. However, there is much for which we should be thankful.

Teachers today are challenging their students to excel in history in ways that make them accountable for their own learning as well as providing them with the glue that is needed to hold a democratic society together. The fact that national and state standards of history education are being addressed is important. The rising tide in teacher-training programs to assist future teachers create active learning environments for their students is a real blessing. We should view both as mutually compatible and not as diametrically opposed.

Abraham Lincoln made a most astute assessment of human nature when he declared, "You will go a lot further with a drop of honey than a jar of vinegar." Try to follow this maxim in your approach to teaching. I have discovered that much of my success as a teacher is due to how I treat my students and how I carry myself in my school. Even though we teach the subject of history, more importantly we teach human beings—young human beings at that. So don't fail to teach the subject in a humanistic fashion. Below are some guidelines:

- Teach history in a way that allows students to touch and find communion with the past.
- Make dynamic use of films and other visuals.
- Get your students out of the classroom to visit the world around them, and if that's not possible bring the outside into the classroom.
- Network extensively and extend yourself beyond your classroom into the community.
- Teach history as narrative and the human experience.
- Model your own quest for knowledge to your students and colleagues.
- Provide students with food for thought about all kinds of historical questions and issues in an effort to build their critical-thinking skills.
- Enjoy your role as a teacher and the relationships you build with everyone you encounter.

Clearly, a dynamic approach to presenting the past to our students can provide them with not only the story of what, why, and who have gone before us, while permitting them to discover their own place in the pageant of the human experience, but it can open our students to a world of opportunities never before imagined. Students will come away from your classes with a recognition that studying the past is indeed a window to the present as well as offering a greater understanding of themselves. And thus the prophetic voice of Henry Adams finds itself married to the vision of Clio's call.

Appendix A

Resources for Topics Discussed in the Text

American Ex–Prisoners of War
National Capital Office
1120 Vermont Avenue, NW
Washington, D.C. 20412–1111
(202) 418-4258

Andersonville National Historic Site
Route 1, Box 85
Andersonville, Georgia 31711
(912) 924-0343
http://www.nps.gov/ande

The Augustus Saint-Gaudens Memorial
17 East 47th Street
New York, New York 10017
(212) 750-3690

Brookgreen Gardens
P.O. Box 3368
Pawleys Island, South Carolina
   29585–3368
(843) 237-4218

Chesterwood
The Home and Studio of Daniel
   Chester French
P.O. Box 827
Stockbridge, Massachusetts 01262
(413) 298-3579

The Civil War Trust
201 Wilson Boulevard
Suite 1120
Arlington, Virginia 22201
(703) 312-7594
http://www.CivilWar.org

Fairmount Park Association
1616 Walnut Street
Suite 2012
Philadelphia, Pennsylvania 19103–5313
(215) 546-7550

Florentine Films
P.O. Box 613
Walpole, New Hampshire 03608
(603) 756-3038

Gettysburg National Military Park
Gettysburg, Pennsylvania 17325
(717) 334-1124
http://www.nps.gov/gett

Kim and Reggie Harris
P.O. Box 18871
Philadelphia, Pennsylvania 19119
(215) 548-1679
Artist Representative: Vivien Niwes
V.N.I., Inc
200 South Wilcox
P.O. Box 436
Castle Rock, Colorado 80104
(303) 814-1500 or (908) 788-5000

Index of American Sculpture
University of Delaware
Art History Department
318 Old College
Newark, Delaware 19716
(302) 831-8415
http://www.seurat.art.udel.edu

Inventory of American Sculpture
601 Indiana Avenue, NW
Suite 300 MRC 230
Smithsonian Institution
Washington, D.C. 20560
(202) 357-2941
http://www.siris.si.edu

Jackdaw Publications
P.O. Box 503
Amawalk, New York 10501
(914) 962-6911

Metropolitan Museum of Art
American Wing
5th Avenue and 82nd Street
New York, New York 10028
(212) 879-5500
http://www.metmuseum.org

National Archives Education Staff
National Archives and Records
    Adminstration
NWE
Washington, D.C. 20408
http://www.nara.gov/education
(202) 501-6172

The National D-Day Memorial
    Foundation
P.O. Box 77
Bedford, Virginia 24523
(800) 351-DDAY
http://www.dday.org

National Gallery of Art
Education Department and Teacher
    Programs
Washington, D.C. 20565
(202) 842-6249
http://www.nga.gov

National Museum of American Art
Smithsonian Institution
Washington, D.C. 20560

(202) 357-2504
http://www.nmaa.si.edu

National Museum of American History
Smithsonian Institution
Washington, D.C. 20565
(202) 357-2500
http://www.si.edu.nmah

National Sculpture Society
1177 Avenue of the Americas
15th Floor
New York, New York 10033
(212) 764-5645
http://www.sculptor.org/nss

Oklahoma City National Memorial
    Foundation
P.O. Box 323
One Leadership Square
Suite 150
Oklahoma City, Oklahoma 73101
(405) 235-3313
http://connections.oklahoma.net/
memorial

Pioneer Woman Museum
701 Monument Street
Ponca City, Oklahoma 74604
(405) 765-6108

Saint-Gaudens National Historic Site
RR #2, P.O. Box 73
Cornish, New Hampshire 03745
(603) 675-2175
http://www.nps.gov/saga

Save Outdoor Sculpture Project
Heritage Preservation
1730 K Street, NW
Suite 566
Washington, D.C. 20006–3836
(202) 634-1422
http://www.heritagepreservation.org

Appendix B

History Films

Hollywood Motion Pictures

American Graffiti. Producer: George Lucas; Director: George Lucas. 120 minutes. Universal Pictures, 1972, videocassette.

Amistad. Producers: Steven Spielberg, et al.; Director: Steven Spielberg. 152 minutes. Dreamworks, SKG, 1997, videocassette.

Andersonville. Producer: David W. Rintels; Director: John Frankenheimer. 168 minutes. Turner Network Television, 1995, videocassette.

Andersonville Trial. Producer: Lewis Freedman; Director: George C. Scott. 150 minutes. KCET, Los Angeles, 1970, videocassette.

The Best Years of Our Lives. Producer: Samuel Goldwyn; Director: William Wyler. 172 minutes. RKO, 1946, videocassette.

Birth of a Nation. Producer: David W. Griffith; Director: David W. Griffith. 190 minutes. David W. Griffith Corporation, 1915, videocassette.

The Buccaneer. Producer: Henry Wilcoxon; Director: Anthony Quinn. 121 minutes. Paramount Pictures, 1958, videocassette.

Crisis at Central High. Producers: Paul Levinson, et al.; Director: Lamont Johnson. 120 minutes. CBS Entertainment Productions, 1981, videocassette.

The Day the Earth Stood Still. Producer: Julian Blaustein; Director: Robert Wise, 92 minutes. Twentieth Century Fox, 1951, videocassette.

Dr. Strangelove. Producer: Stanley Kubrick; Director: Stanley Kubrick. 102 minutes. Hawk, 1963, videocassette.

Gettysburg. Producers: Robert Katz and Moctesuma Esparza; Director: Ronald Maxwell. 254 minutes. Turner Pictures, 1993, videocassette.

Glory. Producer: Freddie Fields; Director: Edward Zwick. 122 minutes. Tri-Star, 1989, videocassette.

Gone with the Wind. Producer: David O. Selznick; Director: Victor Flemming, et. al. 220 minutes. Selznick International Pictures, 1939, videocassette.

I Will Fight No More Forever. Producer: Stan Margulies; Director: Richard T. Heffren. 105 minutes. Wolper Productions, 1975, videocassette.

The Long Walk Home. Producer: Howard W. Kotch, Jr.; Director: Richard Pearce. 97 minutes. Miramax, 1990, videocassette.

The Longest Day. Producer: Daryl F. Zanuck; Directors: Andrew Marton, Ken Annakin, and Bernhard Wicki. 180 minutes. Twentieth Century Fox, 1962, videocassette.

Modern Times. Producer: Charles Chaplin; Director: Charles Chaplin. 85 minutes. United Artists, 1936.

Rosewood. Producer: Tracey Barone; Director: John Singleton. 140 minutes. Warner Brothers, 1997, videocassette.

Schindler's List. Producer: Steven Spielberg; Director: Steven Spielberg. 197 minutes. Universal Pictures, 1993, videocassette.

Sergeant York. Producers: Jesse L. Lasky and Hal B. Wallis; Director: Howard Hawks. 137 minutes. Warner Brothers, 1941, videocassette.

Tora, Tora, Tora. Producer: Elmo Williams; Directors: Richard Fleischer, Toshio Masuda, and Kinji Fukasaku. 143 minutes. Twentieth Century Fox, 1970, videocassette.

For a more complete list of related Hollywood History films consult the books *American History on the Screen* by Wendy S. Wilson and Gerald H. Herman and *Past Imperfect: History According to the Movies* edited by Mark C. Carnes. Both sources are listed in the references.

Documentaries

America by Design: Episode 4: Public Places and Monuments. Producer: Charles Guggenheim and WTTW/Chicago. 60 minutes. 1987, videocassette.

The American Experience Series. For additional information contact: PBS Video, 1320 Braddock Place, Alexandria, Virginia 22314, (703) 739-5000, (703) 739-5400.

A Time for Justice: America's Civil Rights Movement. Producer: Charles Guggenheim. 38 minutes. Teaching Tolerance, 1992, videocassette.

Augustus Saint-Gaudens: An American Original. Producer: Paul G. Sanderson. 28 minutes. Our Town Films, 1985, videocassette.

Baseball. Producers: Ken Burns and Lynn Novick. 1,080 minutes. The Baseball Film Project, 1994, videocassette.

Brooklyn Bridge. Producer: Ken Burns. 60 minutes. Florentine Films, 1984, videocassette.

The Civil War. Producers: Ken and Ric Burns. 860 minutes. Florentine Films, 1990, videocassette.

Civil War Journal: War Crimes—The Death Camps. Producer: Craig Haffner. 48 minutes. Greystone Communications, 1995, videocassette.

Civil War Journal: Battlefield Medicine. Producers: Craig Haffner and Donna E. Lusitana. 48 minutes. Greystone Communications, 1994, videocassette.

D-Day. Producer: Charles Guggenheim. 60 minutes. Guggenheim Productions, 1994, videocassette.

The Donner Party. Producers: Lisa Ades and Ric Burns. 81 minutes. Steeplechase Films, 1992, videocassette.

Echoes of Captivity. Producer: Polly Wiester. 43 minutes. Friends of Andersonville, 1998, videocassette.

Frederick Douglass: When the Lion Wrote History. Producer: Orlando Bagwell. 90 minutes. Rosa Productions, 1994, videocassette.

George Washington: The Man Who Wouldn't Be King. Producer: Donald Sutherland. 60 minutes. PBS Productions, 1992, videocassette.

Glory—The True Story of Glory Continues. Producer: Ray Herbeck, Jr. 30 minutes. Tri-Star Pictures, 1991, videocassette.

Great American Speeches: 80 Years of Political Oratory. Producer: Parker Payson. 240 minutes. Pieri and Springs Production, 1995, videocassette.

Ida B. Wells—A Passion for Justice. Producer: William Greaves and Louise Archambault. 60 minutes. William Greaves Productions, 1989, videocassette.

In the White Man's Image. Producers: Christine Lesiak and Matt Jones. 60 minutes. Native American Public Broadcasting and the Nebraska Educational Network, 1991, videocassette.

The Johnstown Flood. Producer: Charles Guggenheim. 53 minutes. Guggenheim Productions, 1989, videocassette.

Lincoln. Producers: Peter W. Kunhardt and Philip B. Kunhardt, Jr. 240 minutes. Kunhardt Productions, 1992, videocassette.

The Massachusetts 54th Colored Infantry. Producer: Jacqueline Shearer. 60 minutes. Reel Deal Productions, 1990, videocassette.

Public Sculpture: America's Legacy. Producer: Robert Pierce. 28 minutes. National Museum of American Art: Smithsonian Institution, 1995, videocassette.

Saint-Gaudens: Masque of the Golden Bowl. Producer: T.W. Timreck. 60 minutes. Metropolitan Museum of Art, 1986, videocassette.

The Shadow of Hate: A History of Intolerance in America. Producer: Charles Guggenheim. 40 minutes. Teaching Tolerance, 1995, videocassette.

Songs of the Civil War. Producers: Jim Brown and Ken Burns. 60 minutes. Ginger Group Productions and American Documentaries, 1991, videocassette.

The Speeches of Abraham Lincoln. Producer: Matthew White. 45 minutes. MPI Home Video, 1990, videocassette.

The Statue of Liberty. Producer: Ken Burns. 60 minutes. Florentine Films, 1985, videocassette.

The Stonecarvers. Producers: Paul Wagner and Marjorie Hunt. 29 minutes. Washington Area Film/Video League, 1984, videocassette.

The Story of Andersonville. Producer: Wells Communication. 30 minutes. 1992, videocassette.

Wax Blood. Bronze Skin. Producer: T.W. Timreck. 26 minutes. Spofford Films, 1994, videocassette.

Appendix C

Related Websites

U.S. History

Archiving Early America
http://earlyamerica.com/

Declaration of Independence Exhibit
http://lcweb.loc.gov/exhibits/declara/declara1.html

Explore the West from Monticello (Lewis & Clark Exhibit)
http://www.lib.virginia.edu/exhibits/lewis_clark/home.html

The Federalist Papers
http://www.law.uoknor.edu/histfederalist.html

From American Revolution to Reconstruction
http://www.let.rug.nl/~welling/usa/revolution.html

The Historical Text Archive
http://www.msstate.edu/Archives/History/index.html

Historic Documents
http://www.ukans.edu/carrie/docs/docs_us.html

U.S. Historical Documents
http://www.law.uoknor.edu/ushist.html

African-American History

African-American History Site
http://www.afroam.org/index.html

Atlanta's King Center
http://www.thekingcenter.com

Frederick Douglass Web Site
http://www.history.rochester.edu/class/-DOUGLASS/home.html

Rosa Parks Web Page
http://www.grandtimes.com/rosa.html

World Book's African American Journey
http://www.worldbook.com/features/blackhistory/index.html

Libraries and Museums

Home Page: American Memory from the Library of Congress
http://lcweb2.loc.gov/ammem/ammemhome.html

Library of Congress Exhibits
http://lcweb.loc.gov/exhibits

Library of Congress World Wide Web Home Page
http://lcweb.loc.gov/

Movietone News Online
http://www.iguide.com/movies/movietone

Museum of Fine Arts
http://www.mfa.org/

National Museum of the American Indian
http://www.si.edu/nmai/

Prints and Photographs: An Illustrated Guide of the Library of Congress
http://lcweb.loc.gov/coll/print/guide

Smithsonian Institution
http://www.si.edu/

Television

Discovery Channel Online
http://www.discovery.com/

The History Channel's Today in History
http://www.historychannel.com/today

PBS Online
http://www.pbs.org

WGBH Educational Foundation
http://www.boston.com/wgbh/

Civil War Web Sites

1861–1865 World Wide Web Information Archive, Civil War Sites
http://www.access.digex.net/~bdboyle/cw.html

Civil War Women Archival Collection of Duke University
http://scriptorium.lib.duke.edu/collections/civil-war-women.html

Jewish American History, Jews in the Civil War
http://www.geocities.com/Athens/Forum/1867/jewish.html

The Joshua Lawrence Chamberlain Page
http://www.ma.ultranet.com/~maineiac/jlc.html

Joshua Lawrence Chamberlain
http://www.cooper.edu/~goldma/chamberlain.html

Letters from an Iowa Civil War Soldier
http:www.ucsc.edu/civil-war-letters/home.html

Library of Congress (Do a search for Civil War and get many interesting things from photos to oral histories.)
http://rs6.loc.gov/amhome.html

Maine State Archives Civil War Page
http://www.state.me.us/sos/arc/archives/military/civilwar/civilwar.html

Making of America Digital Library
http://www.umdl.umich.edu/moa

National Parks Service *Links to the Past*
http://www.cr.nps.gov/

North Star's Underground Railroad Learning Center
http://www.ugrr.org/learn/learn.html

United States Civil War Center
http://www.cwc.lsu.edu/civlink.html

Valley of the Shadows
http://jefferson.village.virginia.edu/vshadow/vshadow.html

Other Web Sites with Teacher Resources

National Archives Digital Classroom
http://www.nara.gov/education/classrm.html

National History Day
http://www.Thehistorynet.com/NationalHistoryDay/

National Park Service's The Learning Place
http:www.ustc.org/resource.html

Lyric Server Web Sites

The Digital Tradition of Folk Song Database
http://www.deltablues.com/folksearch.html

Music and Oldies Resources From Nerd World Media
http://www.nerdworld.com/nw9863.html

The Song Index
http://206.114.73.124/songindx/refsong.html

Appendix D

History Education Associations

American Association for State and Local History
Terry L. Davis, Executive Director and CEO
530 Church Street, Suite 600
Nashville, TN 37219–9325
phone: (615) 255-2971
fax: (615) 255-2972
email: aaslh@aaslh.org
website: http://www.aaslh.org

American Historical Association
Sandria Freitag, Executive Director
400 A. Street, SE
Washington, D.C. 20003
phone: (202) 544-2422
fax: (202) 544-8307
website: http://chnm.gmu.edu/aha

American Studies Association
John F. Stevens, Executive Director
1120 19th St. NW, Suite 301
Washington, D.C. 20036
phone: (202) 467-4783
fax: (202) 467-4786
email: pp001366@mindspring.com, asastaff@erols.com
website: http://www.georgetown.edu/crossroads

History Teaching Alliance
Loretta Sullivan Lobes, Director
Department of History
240 Baker Hall
Carnegie Mellon University
Pittsburgh, PA 15213
phone: (412) 268-1143

fax: (412) 268-1019
email: lllj@andrew.cmu.edu
website: http://hss.cmu.edu/nhen

National Archives and Records Administration
Paula Nassen Poulos
Public Programs (NWE)
Washington, D.C. 20408
phone: (202) 501-5210
fax: (202) 219-1888
email: paula.poulos@arch1.nara.gov
website: http://www.nara.gov

National Center for History in the Schools
Gary B. Nash, Director
University of California, Los Angeles
1100 Glendon Ave., Suite 927
Box 951588
Los Angeles, CA 90095–1588
fax: (310) 794-6740
email: gnash@ucla.edu

National Council for History Education
Elaine Wrisley Reed, Executive Director
26915 Westwood Rd., Suite B-2
Westlake, OH 44145
phone: (216) 835-1776
fax: (215) 835-1295
email: nche19@mail.idt.net
website: http://www.history.org/nche

National Council on Public History
David G. Vanderstel, Director
327 Cavanaugh Hall—IUPUI
425 University Blvd.
Indianapolis, IN 46202–5140
phone: (317) 274-2716
fax: (317) 274-2347

National Council for the Social Studies
Martharose Laffey, Executive Director
3501 Newark St. NW
Washington D.C. 20016
phone: (202) 966-7840
fax: (202) 966-2061
email: ncss@ncss.org

National History Day
Cathy Gorn, Executive Director
0119 Cecil Hall
University of Maryland, College Park
College Park, MD 20742

phone: (301) 314-9739
fax: (301) 314-9767
email: hstryday@aol.com
website: http://www.thehistorynet.com/NationalHistoryDay

National Park Service
Dwight T. Pitcaithley, Chief Historian
1849 C Street NW, Room NC400
Washington, D.C. 20240
phone: (202) 343-8167
fax: (202) 343-1244
email: Dwight_Pitcaithley@nps.gov
website: http://www.nps.gov

National Register of Historic Places
Beth M. Boland, Historian
Teaching with Historic Places
National Register, History and Education Division
National Park Service
1849 C Street NW, Suite 400
Washington, D.C. 20240
phone: (202) 343-9545
fax: (202) 343-1836
email: Beth_Boland@nps.gov
website: http://www.cr.nps.gov/nr/twhp/home.html

Organization of American Historians
Arnita A. Jones, Executive Secretary
112 North Bryan Street
Bloomington, IN 47408–4199
phone: (812) 855-7311
fax: (812) 855-0696
email: arnjones@indiana.edu
website: http://www.indiana.edu/~oah

Organization of History Teachers
Gloria Sesso
19 Corie Court
Port Jefferson, NY 11777
phone: (516) 421-6575 or (516) 473-6119
fax: (516) 331-1625

References

Abdul-Jabbar, Kareem. 1996. *Black Profiles in Courage: A Legacy of African American Achievement.* New York: William Morrow Company.

Adler, Mortimer J. and Charles Van Doren. 1972. *How to Read a Book.* New York: Simon and Schuster.

Ambrose, Stephen E. 1994. *D-Day, June 6, 1944: The Climactic Battle of World War II.* New York: Simon and Schuster.

————. 1997. *Citizen Soldiers.* New York: Simon and Schuster.

Armstrong, Tom, Wayne Craven, Norman Feder, Barabara Haskell, Rosiland E. Krauss, Daniel Robbins, and Marcia Tucker. 1976. *200 Years of American Sculpture.* New York: Whitney Museum of Art.

Ayres, William, ed. 1993. *Picturing History: American Painting 1770–1930.* New York: Rizzoli.

Bach, Ira J. and Mary Lackritz Gray. 1983. *A Guide to Chicago's Public Sculpture.* Chicago: University of Chicago Press.

Bach, Penny Balkin. 1992. *Public Art in Philadelphia.* Philadelphia: Temple University Press.

Baigell, Matthew. 1984. *A Concise History of American Painting and Sculpture.* New York: Harper and Row.

Balkoski, Joseph. 1989. *Beyond the Beachhead: The 29th Division in Normandy.* Harrisburg: Stackpole Books.

Benson, Richard and Lincoln Kirstein. 1973. *Lay this Laurel.* New York: Eakins Press.

Blockson, Charles. 1987. *The Underground Railroad.* New York: Prentice Hall.

Boime, Albert. 1990. *The Art of Exclusion: Representing Blacks in the Nineteenth Century.* Washington: Smithsonian.

Boorstein, Daniel. 1958. *The Americans: The Colonial Experience.* New York: Random House.

————. 1965. *The Americans: The National Experience.* New York: Random House.

————. 1973. *The Americans: The Democratic Experience.* New York: Random House.

Briley, Ron. 1990. "Reel History: U.S. History 1932–1972, as Viewed Through the Lens of Hollywood," In *The History Teacher* 23 (May): 215–236.

————. 1994. "Reel History and the Cold War," In *The OAH Magazine of History.* (Winter): 19–23.

————. 1996. "The Hollywood Feature as Historical Artifact." In *Film and History* (Vol. 26, No. 1–4): 82–84.

Brinkley, Douglas. 1993. *The Majic Bus: An American Odyssey.* San Diego: Harcourt Brace and Company.

Brooklyn Museum. 1979. *The American Renaissance: 1876–1917.* New York: The Brooklyn Museum.

Building a United States History Curriculum. 1997. Westlake: The National Council for History Education.

Burchard, Peter. 1965. *One Gallant Rush: Robert Gould Shaw and His Brave Black Regiment.* New York: St. Martin's Press.

Burkholder, J. Peter. 1995. *All Made of Tunes: Charles Ives and the Uses of Musical Borrowing.* New Haven: Yale University Press.

Buscaglia, Leo. 1982. *Living, Loving and Learning.* New York: Ballantine.

Butcher, Russell D. 1997. *Exploring Our National Historic Parks and Sites.* Niwot: Roberts Rinehart.

Carlock, Marty. 1993. *A Guide to Public Art in Greater Boston.* Boston: Harvard Common Press.

Carnes, Mark C. ed. 1995. *Past Imperfect: History According to the Movies.* New York: Henry Holt.

Cohen, Barbara. 1997. *Social Studies Resources on the Internet: A Guide for Teachers.* Portsmouth: Heinemann.

Coles, Robert. 1997. *The Moral Intelligence of Children.* New York: Random House.

The Complete Guide to America's National Parks. 1998. New York: Fodor's Travel Publications.

Convis, Charles L. 1997. *Pioneer Women.* Carson City: Pioneer Press.

Cooke, Alistair. 1973. *Alistair Cooke's America.* New York: Alfred A. Knopf.

Copland, Aaron and Vivian Perlis. 1984. *Copland: 1900–1942.* New York: St. Martin's Press/Marek.

————. 1984. *Since 1943.* New York: St. Martin's Press/Marek.

Craven, Wayne. 1984. *Sculpture in America.* Newark: University of Delaware Press.

Cronkite, Walter. 1996. *A Reporter's Life.* New York: Alfred A. Knopf.

DeGalan, Julie and Stephen Lambert. 1995. *Great Jobs for History Majors.* New York: VGM Career Horizons.

Donald, David Herbert. 1995. *Lincoln.* New York: Simon and Schuster.

Doyle, Robert C. 1994. *Voices from Captivity: Interpreting the American POW Narrative.* Lawrence: University Press of Kansas.

Drake, Frederick D. and Lawrence W. McBride. 1997. "Reinvigorating the Teaching of History through Alternative Assessment." In *The History Teacher,* (Volume 30, No. 2): 145–173.

Drez, Ronald J. 1994. *Voices of D-Day: The Story of the Allied Invasion Told by Those Who Were There.* Baton Rouge: Louisiana State University Press.

Dryfhout, John H. 1982. *The Work of Augustus Saint-Gaudens*. Hanover: University Press of New England.

Ellis, Jerry. 1991. *Walking the Trail: One Man's Journey Along the Cherokee Trail of Tears*. New York: Delacorte Press.

———. 1993. *Bareback: One Man's Journey Along the Pony Express Trail*. New York: Delacorte Press.

———. 1995. *Marching Through Georgia: My Walk with Sherman*. New York: Delacorte Press.

Emilio, Luis F. 1992. *A Brave Black Regiment*. New York: Bantam.

Exton, Peter and Dorsey Kleitz. 1985. *Milestones into Headstones: Mini Biographies of Fifty Fascinating Americans Buried in Washington, D.C.* McLean: EPM Publishing.

Fairfax County Public Schools. 1998. *Virginia and United States History Program of Studies*. Fairfax Office of Instructional Services.

Forten, Charlotte. 1981. *The Journal of Charlotte Forten*. Edited with an introduction by Ray Allen Billington. New York: Norton.

Francis, Rell G. 1976. *Cyrus E. Dallin: Let Justice Be Done*. Springville: Springville Museum of Art.

Franklin, John Hope. 1994. *From Slavery to Freedom: A History of Negro Americans*. New York: McGraw-Hill.

Frassanito, William A. 1975. *Gettysburg: A Journey in Time*. New York: Charles Scribner's Sons.

———. 1978. *Antietam: The Photographic Legacy of America's Bloodiest Day*. New York: Charles Scribner's Sons.

Freeman, David B. 1997. *Carved in Stone: The History of Stone Mountain*. Macon: Mercer University Press.

Futch, Ovid L. 1968. *History of Andersonville Prison*. Florida: University of Florida.

Gagnon, Paul, ed. 1991. *Historical Literacy: The Case for History in American Education*. Boston: Houghton Mifflin.

Gardner, Howard. 1983. *Frames of Mind: The Theory of Multiple Intelligences*. New York: Basic Books.

———. 1993. *Multiple Intelligences: The Theory in Practice*. New York: Basic Books.

Gayle, Margot and Michele Cohen. 1988. *Guide to Manhattan's Outdoor Sculpture*. New York: Prentice Hall.

Gilbert, Bill. 1992. *They Also Served: Baseball and the Homefront, 1941–1945*. New York: Crown Publishing.

Gillis, John R. ed. 1994. *Commemorations: The Politics of National Identity*. Princeton: Princeton University Press.

Glatthaar, Joseph T. 1990. *Forged in Battle: The Civil War Alliance of Black Soldiers and White Officers*. New York: Free Press.

Goldman, Daniel. 1995. *Emotional Intelligence*. New York: Bantam Books.

Gooding, James Henry. 1991. *On the Altar of Freedom: A Black Soldier's Civil War Letters from the Front.* Edited by Virginia M. Adams. Amherst: University of Massachusetts.

Greenthal, Kathryn. 1985. *Augustus Saint-Gaudens: Master Sculptor.* New York: Metropolitan Museum of Art.

Halberstam, David. 1989. *Summer of 49.* New York: William Morrow and Company.

Hansen, Chadwick. 1975. "The 54th Massachusetts Black Infantry in Art." In *The Massachusetts Review* (Volume 16, No. 4): 745–759. Amherst: University of Massachusetts.

Hartwig, D. Scott. 1996. *A Killer Angels Companion.* Gettysburg: Thomas Publications.

Hendricks, Patricia D. and Becky Duval Reese. 1989. *A Century of Sculpture in Texas: 1889–1989.* Austin: University of Texas.

Hersey, John. 1946, 1989 ed. *Hiroshima.* New York: Viking.

Hillman, James. 1996. *The Soul's Code: In Search of Character and Calling.* New York: Random House.

Holt, Tom. 1990. *Thinking Historically: Narrative, Imagination and Understanding.* New York: The College Board.

Holzer, Harold and Mark E. Neely, Jr. 1993. *Mine Eyes Have Seen the Glory: The Civil War in Art.* New York: Orion Books.

Howe, Harold. 1997. *Service Learning.* Chicago: University of Chicago Press.

Jackson, Donald C. 1988. *Great American Bridges and Dams.* Washington: The Preservation Press.

Kammen, Michael. 1997. *In the Past Lane: Historical Perspectives on American Culture.* New York: Oxford University Press.

———. 1991. *Mystic Chords of Memory: The Transformation of Tradition in American Culture.* New York: Alfred A. Knopf.

Kaplan, Sidney. 1988. "The Sculptural World of Augustus Saint-Gaudens." In *Massachusetts Review* (Volume 30, No. 1): 17–64. Amherst: University of Massachusetts.

Kinnard, Roy. 1996. *The Blue and the Gray on the Silver Screen: More than 80 Years of Civil War Movies.* Secaucus: Birch Lane Press.

Kirstein, Lincoln and Jerry L. Thompson. 1989. *Memorial to a Marriage.* New York: Metropolitan Museum of Art.

Kobrin, David. 1996. *Beyond the Textbook: Teaching History Using Documents and Primary Sources.* Portsmouth: Heinemann.

Kostoff, Spiro. 1987. *America by Design.* New York: Oxford University Press.

LaPierre, Yvette. 1996. *America's Monuments, Memorials, and Historic Sites.* Lincolnwood: Publications International, Ltd.

Leckie, William H. 1967. *The Buffalo Soldiers: A Narrative of the Negro Cavalry in the West.* Norman: University of Oklahoma Press.

Linenthal, Edward T. 1991. *Sacred Ground: Americans and Their Battlefields*. Urbana: University of Illinois Press.

———. 1995. *Preserving Memory: The Struggle to Create America's Holocaust Museum*. New York: Viking.

Linenthal, Edward T. and Tom Engelhardt. 1996. *History Wars: The Enola Gay and Other Battles for the American Past*. New York: Metropolitan Books.

Little, Carol Morris. 1996. *A Comprehensive Guide to Outdoor Sculpture in Texas*. Austin: University of Texas Press.

Loewen, James W. 1995. *Lies My Teacher Told Me*. New York: New Press.

Lowell, Robert. 1964. *For the Union Dead*. New York: Farrar, Straus & Giroux.

Luvaas, Jay and Harold W. Nelson, eds. 1986. *The U.S. Army War College Guide to the Battle of Gettysburg*. Carlisle: South Mountain Press.

Marvel, William. 1994. *Andersonville: The Last Depot*. Chapel Hill: University of North Carolina Press.

McCormick, Floyd G. 1994. *The Power of Positive Teaching*. Melbourne: Krieger Publishing.

McCullough, David. 1968. *The Johnstown Flood*. New York: Simon and Schuster.

———. 1972. *The Great Bridge*. New York: Simon and Schuster.

———. 1992. *Brave Companions: Portraits in History*. New York: Simon and Schuster.

McPherson, James M. 1991. *The Negro's Civil War*. New York: Ballantine.

Medved, Michael. 1992. *Hollywood vs. America*. New York: Harper Collins.

Metcalf, Fay D. and Matthew T. Downey. 1982. *Using Local History in the Classroom*. Nashville: American Association for State and Local History.

Michener, James A. 1996. *This Noble Land: My Vision for America*. New York: Random House.

Miller, Russell. 1993. *Nothing Less than Victory: The Oral History of D-Day*. New York: William Morrow and Company.

Moe, Richard. 1993. *The Last Full Measure: The Life and Death of the First Minnesota Volunteers*. New York: Henry Holt and Company.

Moon, William Least Heat. 1982. *Blue Highways: A Journey into America*. New York: Random House.

Nash, Gary, Charlotte Crabtree and Ross E. Dunn. 1997. *History On Trial: Culture Wars and the Teaching of the Past*. New York: Alfred A. Knopf.

National Standards for United States History: Exploring the American Experience. 1996. Los Angeles: National Center for History in the Schools.

Oates, Stephen B. *With Malice Toward None: A Life of Abraham Lincoln*. 1977. New York: Harper and Row.

O'Reilley, Mary Rose. 1998. *Radical Presence: Teaching as Contemplative Practice*. Portsmouth: Boynton/Cook.

Palmer, Laura. 1987. *Shrapnel in the Heart: Letters and Remembrances from the Vietnam Veterans Memorial*. New York: Random House.

Pember, Phoebe Yates. 1954. *A Southern Woman's Story: Life in Confederate Richmond.* Edited by Bell I. Wiley. Marietta: Mockingbird Books.

Percoco, James A. 1995. *Using Primary Sources: A Guide for Teachers and Parents.* Woodbridge: Primary Source Media.

Percoco, James A. and Michael Richman. 1998. *Commemorative Sculpture in the United States: A Unit of Study for Grades 9–12.* Los Angeles: National Center for History in the Schools and Organization of American Historians.

Perret, Geoffrey. 1989. *A Country Made by War.* New York: Random House.

Peterson, Merrill D. 1994. *Lincoln in American Memory.* New York: Oxford University Press.

Pickles, Tim. 1993. *New Orleans 1815.* London: Osprey.

Piehler, G. Kurt. 1995. *Remembering War the American Way: 1783–Present.* Washington: Smithsonian.

Postman, Neil. 1995. *The End of Education: Redefining the Value of School.* New York. Random House.

Ransom, John. 1963. *John Ransom's Andersonville Diary.* Middlebury: Paul S. Eriksson.

Richman, Michael. 1976. *Daniel Chester French: An American Sculptor.* Washington: The Preservation Press.

Ritchie, Donald A. 1995. *Doing Oral History.* New York: Twayne Publishers.

Rollins, Peter C. 1983. *Hollywood as Historian: American Film in a Cultural Context.* Lexington: The University Press of Kentucky.

Roy, Andrew. 1996. *Fallen Soldier: Memoir of a Civil War Casualty.* Edited by William J. Miller. Montgomery: Elliot and Clark.

Ryan, Cornelius. 1959. *The Longest Day.* New York: Simon and Schuster.

Savage, Beth L. ed. 1994. *African American Historic Places.* Washington: Preservation Press.

Savage, Kirk. 1997. *Standing Soldiers, Kneeling Slaves: Race, War, and Monument in Nineteenth-Century America.* Princeton: Princeton University Press.

Saxon, Lyle. 1930. *Lafitte the Pirate.* New York: Century Company.

Schlereth, Thomas J. 1980. *Artifacts and the American Past.* Nashville: American Association for State and Local History.

Schlesinger, Arthur. 1992. *The Disuniting of America.* New York: Norton.

Shaara, Michael. 1974. *The Killer Angels.* New York: David McKay Company.

Shapiro, Mary J. 1983. *A Picture History of the Brooklyn Bridge.* New York: Dover.

The Shaw Memorial: A Celebration of an American Masterpiece. 1997. Conshohocken: Eastern National.

Shaw, Robert Gould. 1992. *Blue-Eyed Child of Fortune: The Civil War Letters of Robert Gould Shaw.* Edited by Russell Duncan. Athens: University of Georgia Press.

Speer, Lonnie R. 1997. *Portals to Hell: Military Prisons of the Civil War.* Mechanicsburg: Stackpole Books.

Steffens, Henry J. 1988. "Collaborative Learning in a History Seminar," In *The History Teacher* (Vol. 21, No. 10): 3–11.

———. 1988. "Journals in the Teaching of History." In *The Journal Book,* edited by Toby Fulwiler. Portsmouth: Boynton/Cook.

———. 1988. "Students Writing to Learn." In *The OAH Council of Chairs Newsletter.* (June): 11–14.

Steffens, Henry J. and Mary Jane Dickerson. 1988. *Writers Guide to History.* Lexington: D.C. Heath.

Stevens, Joseph E. 1990. *America's National Battlefield Parks.* Norman: University of Oklahoma Press.

Stewart, George R. 1959. *Pickett's Charge.* Boston: Houghton.

———. 1960. *Ordeal by Hunger: The Story of the Donner Party.* Boston: Houghton.

Stratton, Joanna L. 1981. *Pioneer Women.* New York: Simon and Schuster.

Swaford, Jan. 1996. *Charles Ives: A Life with Music.* New York: W.W. Norton and Company.

Taft, Lorado. 1903. *The History of American Sculpture.* New York: Arno Press.

Teaching With Documents: Using Primary Sources from the National Archives. 1989. Washington: The National Archives and Records Administration.

Tey, Josephine. 1951. *The Daughter of Time.* New York: Scribner Paperbacks.

Thomas, Benjamin P. 1952. *Abraham Lincoln.* New York: Alfred A. Knopf.

Troiani, Don and Brian C. Pohanka. 1995. *Don Troiani's Civil War.* Mechanicsburg: Stackpole Books.

Tuchman, Barbara W. 1981. *Practicing History.* New York: Alfred A. Knopf.

Tygiel, Jules. 1983. *Baseball's Great Experiment: Jackie Robinson and His Legacy.* New York: Random House.

Viola, Herman J. 1990. *After Columbus: The Smithsonian Chronicle of the North American Indians.* Washington: Smithsonian Books.

Voices of the Civil War: Gettysburg. 1995. Alexandria: Time-Life Books.

Wallace, Mike. 1996. *Mickey Mouse History and Other Essays on American Memory.* Philadelphia: Temple University Press.

Watkins, Sam R. 1962. *"Co. Aytch."* New York: Macmillan.

Wheeler, Richard. 1987. *Witness to Gettysburg.* New York: Harper and Row.

Wilkinson, Burke. 1985. *Uncommon Clay: The Life and Works of Augustus Saint-Gaudens.* San Diego: Harcourt Brace Jovanovich.

Wills, Garry. 1992. *Lincoln at Gettysburg: The Words that Remade America.* New York: Simon and Schuster.

Wilson, Wendy S. and Gerald H. Herman. 1994. *American History on the Screen: A Teacher's Resource Book on Film and Video.* Portland: J. Weston Walch.

Wood, Kathleen Sinclair. 1990. *Clues to American Sculpture.* Washington: Starhill Press.